CURRENCIES AFTER THE CRASH

THE UNCERTAIN FUTURE OF THE GLOBAL PAPER-BASED CURRENCY SYSTEM

EDITED WITH COMMENTARY BY

SARA EISEN

New York   Chicago   San Francisco   Lisbon   London
Madrid   Mexico City   Milan   New Delhi   San Juan
Seoul   Singapore   Sydney   Toronto

1 2 3 4 5 6 7 8 9 10   DOC/DOC   1 8 7 6 5 4 3 2

ISBN   978-0-07-178488-7
MHID   0-07-178488-8

e-ISBN   978-0-07-178489-4
e-MHID   0-07-178489-6

McGraw-Hill books are available at special quantity discounts to use as premiums and sales promotions or for use in corporate training programs. To contact a representative, please e-mail us at bulksales@mcgraw-hill.com.

This book is printed on acid-free paper.

CONTENTS

LIST OF CONTRIBUTORS

Jörg Asmussen
Member of the Executive Board of the European Central Bank
Asmussen is responsible for the Directorate General International and European
Relations and the Directorate General Legal Services at the European Central
Bank. Before joining the ECB, he served in various positions at the German
Federal Ministry of Finance; he was state secretary from 2008 to 2011 and
acted as the chancellor's G-20 sherpa in 2011.

Peter Boockvar
Market Strategist and Portfolio Manager, Miller Tabak + Co.
Boockvar is also president of OCLI, LLC, and OCLI2, LLC, farmland real estate
investment funds, and is a CNBC contributor. He joined Miller Tabak + Co.,
LLC, in 1994 after working in the corporate bond research department at
Donaldson, Lufkin & Jenrette.

Megan Greene
Director of European Economics, Roubini Global Economics
Prior to working as director of European economics at Roubini Global Economics, Greene was the eurozone crisis expert at the Economist Intelligence
Unit, an advisor to the Liechtenstein royal family on eradicating money
laundering from the principality's financial services industry, and an investment banking analyst at JPMorgan.

Stephen L. Jen
Managing Partner at SLJ Macro Partners
Prior to establishing SLJ Macro Partners in April 2011, Jen was a managing
director at BlueGold Capital. He was also previously the global head of currency research at Morgan Stanley, and he spent four years as an economist
with the International Monetary Fund. Jen holds a PhD in economics from
Massachusetts Institute of Technology.

Robert Johnson
Executive Director of the Institute for New Economic Thinking
Johnson is also a senior fellow and director of the Global Finance Project for the
Franklin and Eleanor Roosevelt Institute in New York. A former managing

director at Soros Fund Management specializing in emerging markets, Johnson has served on the United Nations Commission of Experts on Reforms of the International Monetary and Financial System and was chief economist for the Senate Banking Committee and senior economist for the Senate Budget Committee.

Papa N'Diaye
Deputy Division Chief at the International Monetary Fund
N'Diaye is currently covering China. He has worked on several economies at
  the IMF, including Japan, Australia, Hong Kong SAR, and Malaysia.

James Rickards
Author of the national bestseller *Currency Wars: The Making of the Next Global
  Crisis*
Rickards is a counselor, economist, and investment banker and is a partner in
  a hedge fund based in New York City. In 1998, he was the principal nego-
  tiator of the rescue of Long-Term Capital Management by the Federal
  Reserve.

Gary Shilling
Founder of A. Gary Shilling & Co.
Shilling became Merrill Lynch's first chief economist at age 29, before moving
  on to White, Weld and then establishing his own firm in 1978. He was the
  first to recognize the unwinding of inflation in the early 1980s when he pre-
  dicted "the bond rally of a lifetime," which has driven the 30-year Treasury
  yield from 15.21 percent in 1981 to 2.8 percent.

Anoop Singh
Director of the Asia and Pacific Dept. at the International Monetary Fund
Singh has also worked as special advisor to the governor at the Reserve Bank
  of India and has been an adjunct professor at Georgetown University.

John Taylor
CEO and Founder of FX Concepts
Taylor started with the foreign exchange market before the floating era began
  and was instrumental in pushing Citibank to the forefront of the market in
  the 1970s. In 1981, he started FX Concepts, which has grown into one of the
  leading global managers of foreign exchange risk and absolute return strategies. He also serves on the Fed's FX advisory committee as a buy-side representative. In addition, Taylor has founded a Vermont bank, an international
  university, and a global biotech company focused on hemophilia.

FOREWORD

PAUL O'NEILL, FORMER U.S. SECRETARY OF THE TREASURY

The existing conventions and arrangements that form the framework for an ever more interconnected world economy are much like the tectonic plates in the earth's crust, building up stresses and strains until the pressure is relieved by a catastrophic event or the creation of a new world order. It may not be possible for human beings to prevent earthquakes, volcanic eruptions, or other manifestations of movements in the earth's crust, but since the rules that govern the world economic system are man-made, one would think that we should be able to act in anticipation of a potential crisis. We have had many recent warnings of the need for rethinking: the near melt-down to a barter economy in the United States in 2008–2009, the ongoing saga questioning the durability of the euro, and the proliferation of sovereign states living close to the edge of insolvency.

The collection of ideas in this book is a partial foundation for the architectural reinvention of the world economic order.

Essential to this needed rethinking is an open discussion of the possibilities and realities. When I was secretary of the Treasury, I was hammered by the media for saying that a strong dollar is a consequence of a sound fiscal policy, a vibrant economy, and a higher rate of productivity growth than other countries. In essence, a strong dollar is a consequence, not an independent objective. The media and the markets would have none of it; they preferred the Robert Rubin formulation: "Our policy is a strong dollar."

If we don't open up our thought processes, we are doomed to continue as we are, imposing the cost of failed governments, abetted by private banking interests, on the unknowing people of the world.

PREFACE: A SYSTEM ON SHAKY GROUND

SARA EISEN

The dollar remains at the center of global trade, dominates central bank portfolios around the world, and provides a shelter for nervous investors during economic storms. However, there are two sides to the dollar story. The crisis that began in 2007 has highlighted cracks in the dollar-centric international monetary system, resulting in shaken confidence in the dollar. Massive and destructive imbalances, such as the U.S. trade deficit and China's trade surplus, threaten the world economy. Central banks and federal governments alike, including those of the United States, are finding themselves in uncharted territory, having absorbed massive debt to stimulate their economies during the crisis. For instance, in a 2009 G-20 summit, governments around the world pledged an unprecedented $1.1 trillion to tackle the crisis. In addition to stimulus spending by governments (such as the Troubled Asset Relief Program [TARP] in the United States), central banks have been spending trillions in their crisis-fighting efforts. The Fed adopted unorthodox policies such as quantitative easing, in which central banks create money to buy their own bonds—in the Fed's case, U.S. Treasuries—pushing interest rates lower and injecting liquidity into the financial system.

Unfortunately, the goal of relief by both government-instituted stimulus packages and Fed policy can send indebted economies further into crisis. The Fed has bought more than a trillion dollars' worth of Treasuries in quantitative easing; this has sparked a flood of criticism from politicians and world leaders, who argue that a by-product of such policies is a weaker dollar. Weakness of the U.S. dollar, though desirable domestically for growth, undermines confidence in the world's reserve currency and boosts other currency values around the world as a direct, but undesirable, consequence to other nations. As John Connally, former secretary of the Treasury under Richard Nixon, famously said of the dollar, "Our currency, but your problem."

But the dollar's weakness is not exclusively a by-product of quantitative easing. The dollar's value has declined over the past 10 years, predating the recession of 2008. This occurred as the U.S. government issued massive amounts of debt and the euro emerged on the scene. Central banks and reserve managers the world over have accumulated euros as an alternative to holding all their reserves in dollars. At the same time, China and other nations such as Brazil, Russia, and India known as the BRIC nations, emerged as the world's fastest-growing economies and, as a result, leapt to the forefront of global economic decisions. They also have, by virtue of their economic activity, become the world's largest holders of dollars and other foreign currencies. All of these factors, culminating with the financial crisis in 2008, have led many people to question the outsized, and perhaps outdated, role of the United States in the global monetary system. Think about this: the dollar is the currency the world depends on to price everything from vanilla produced in Comoros to precious oil—and this dependence is an issue that is at the forefront of the world stage today.

With the onslaught of the European debt crisis in 2010, driven by nations' excessive borrowing and explosive debt, the questions facing the international monetary system are now even greater and more complicated than ever. Since it was adopted in 1999, the euro has grown to become the second reserve currency to the dollar, meaning that it is the second most widely traded and held currency in the world, in use by 17 nations in Europe. This common currency area has inherent flaws, however, including gaps in competitiveness, language differences, and disparate fiscal policies among the nations that share the euro and the European Central Bank. The debt crisis has highlighted these structural flaws and is leading to questions about the euro's sustainability and viability.

Since 2010, waning confidence in the world's two major currencies, the euro and the dollar, has caused money to pour into faster-growing economies with more sustainable debt loads, including Brazil, Russia, India, China, and other emerging nations. This investment has led their currencies to strengthen, and consequently, we see them resorting to intervention and other policies aimed at weakening their currencies against others to promote domestic exports. This phenomenon, known as competitive devaluation, has the potential to lead to retaliatory action, resulting in trade wars—a highly undesirable and disruptive consequence of such policy. An example is the currency war of the 1930s that resulted from competitive devaluation by the United States, the United Kingdom, and France. During the Great Depression, each attempted to expand its own economy by devaluing its currency in order to maintain exports and reduce trade surpluses. However, the impact on all was negative, and international trade suffered. This history lesson was not lost on the former chief of the International Monetary Fund, Dominique Strauss-Kahn, who warned in 2010, "There is clearly the idea beginning to circulate that currencies can be used as a policy weapon. Translated into action, such an idea would represent a very serious risk to the global recovery."

Now, more than six decades after the world's major nations drafted new rules for the international monetary system in Bretton Woods, New Hampshire, and almost four decades since those rules were severed in favor of a new system, world governments are again debating whether a major shift in the global currency regime is needed. Nobel laureate in economics Joseph Stiglitz maintains, "A new global reserve system is absolutely essential, if we are to restore the global economy to sustained prosperity and stability." And former French president Nicolas Sarkozy, who held the rotating presidency of the G-20 nations in 2011, stated that the international monetary system, which is still based on the supremacy of the dollar ratified in the Bretton Woods Agreement of 1944, when the United States was the only world superpower, is stale. He stated, "My question is: Are we still in 1945? The answer here is, 'no.'" In fact, Sarkozy had pledged to create a new "financial world order," but this goal was thwarted in 2011 by the emergence of the European debt crisis, which has dominated G-20 and other world economic meetings since 2010.

Some experts wonder whether gold should play a role in currency once again. While most economists do not advocate a gold standard, confidence in gold has grown as its price has climbed steadily for decades, further fueling the debate about whether gold has a role to play. In fact, in the fall of 2010, Robert Zoellick, former president of the World Bank, wrote in the *Financial Times*, "The scope of the changes since 1971 certainly matches those between 1945 and 1971 that prompted the shift from Bretton Woods. Although textbooks may view gold as the old money, markets are using gold as an alternative monetary asset today."[1] Finally, it is notable that the major fiat (paper) currencies, based on confidence in governments, are exhibiting a distinct decline while confidence in gold has been on the rise.

Alternatively, in a report issued in February 2011, the International Monetary Fund (IMF) suggested a possible replacement for the dollar as reserve currency, claiming that Special Drawing Rights (SDRs) could help stabilize the financial system. SDRs represent potential claims on the currencies of IMF members; they can be converted into whatever currency a country needs, and at exchange rates based on a basket of international currencies, as opposed to the dollar exclusively.

The following questions will define and dominate world meetings, including those of the G-20, IMF, and other high-profile gatherings of superpowers in the coming years as leaders debate a new world order. These questions are among many others that are tackled in this book: Will the dollar maintain its leadership role in the global economy? What would replace the dollar as the reserve currency? Is there a role for gold? Is there a role for an IMF currency? Will the euro survive? How can leaders restructure the euro to make it more viable as an international reserve currency? How can China reform its exchange rate to make the yuan more tradable in and accessible to the world? Will China's currency dethrone the U.S. dollar as the world's reserve currency? Will currency wars and competitive devaluations escalate into trade wars? What would a Bretton Woods of the future look like?

If ever there was an important time to hear from preeminent scholars and critical voices on these difficult, but approachable, issues, it is now. I have selected a unique and diverse group of authorities to contribute their thoughts. They include economists; researchers who have spent years studying capital flows, reserves, and exchange rates; and an individual who has made a fortune actually trading currencies. Also featured are a central banker and officials of the IMF. These are strong opinion leaders and individuals who have led the debates on specific issues facing the currency market; some of them have driven public policy, and some are actively playing that role.

The world finds itself once again on the brink of major financial systemic change, the direction of which is not yet eminently clear, but which will most certainly affect almost all of us in our lifetimes. Here you can gain perspective on the leading questions that will dominate the next decade or less from experts elucidating the feasibility of various options that are under current or future consideration by world leaders. You may even become inspired to watch the world stage more actively and listen as these issues are deliberated and events unfold in the near future. That is my intent.

BRETTON WOODS AND THE EMERGENCE OF THE U.S. DOLLAR RESERVE SYSTEM

In order to understand the current international monetary system, its challenges, and the questions about its longevity, it is important to understand how today's framework came into being. Currencies as we know them today are fiat, which means that they are paper money, and that the paper possesses no more value than the denomination printed on it. Before a collective multinational decision made money fiat in the 1970s, paper money had been backed by gold. This international financial order, the gold exchange standard, had been established in 1944 in a pact known as the Bretton Woods Agreement, named for the scenic New Hampshire town that hosted an illustrious delegation of world leaders in July of 1944, before the end of World War II. They devised an international monetary system to provide stability to their economies for a postwar world. The Bretton Woods Agreement determined that the U.S. dollar would have value beyond that which was printed on paper, in the form of gold. A fixed amount of gold would therefore be deposited or set aside to represent the value of the U.S. dollars that were printed, and all other currencies in the world would then be pegged, or become valued, relative to the U.S. dollar. This marked the beginning of the dollar's preeminent role in the international world order, a role that had previously been played by the British pound. Bretton Woods also laid the foundation for the International Monetary Fund (IMF) and the International Bank for Reconstruction and Development, now known as the World Bank. The IMF was created to monitor and stabilize exchange rates and lend currencies to nations with trade gaps, whereas the focus of the World Bank is lending to and aiding countries that are in need.

Historically, this was not the first period characterized by a gold standard; however, it is the most recent. By the 1960s, the United States was experiencing difficulty in maintaining its status as the issuer of the world's reserve currency, as it was unable to provide sufficient gold to countries that were demanding it in exchange for their U.S. dollars. Moreover, world leaders recognized that as economies underwent fluctuations in growth, more flexibility in the monetary system was needed. In 1971, President Richard Nixon broke the link between gold and the dollar, marking the end of the Bretton Woods concordance and the beginning of the modern-day fiat currency system, in which the value of the dollar would be backed by nothing physical—like gold—but only by the promise of the U.S. government. It also meant that currencies would float freely, meaning that their value would be allowed to fluctuate against the value of the dollar based on the market. Thus the international reserve currency system, built around the U.S. dollar and confidence in the U.S. government, was born.

The Foreign Exchange Market

When currencies became free-floating in the 1970s, a door opened into a new international trading dimension known as the foreign exchange market. This market enables traders of all types and from all countries to exchange and invest in currencies in a forum outside of government control. The foreign exchange market is the largest and most liquid of all world markets. For that reason alone, if you didn't know anything about it before, it's time to learn.

A few fast facts about this unique market: it is the only market that is open for trading 24 hours every day except weekends, and to illustrate its liquidity, the volume of trading on an average daily basis was $3.98 trillion in 2010, an increase of about 20 percent over the preceding three-year period. Its emergence as the largest exchange market in so short a period has to do with the growth in high-frequency trading and the electronic revolution. This is a market with no central exchange; it is known as an over-the-counter market because traders deal directly with one another in large financial centers.

The major players who trade foreign exchange, or forex, are banks (commercial banks, investment banks, and central banks), corporations, hedge funds, and individuals. There are several reasons to trade. Banks can trade simply to make a profit. Corporations like McDonald's, which receive a large portion of their sales from outside the United States in foreign currencies, can trade to hedge their overseas exposure, so that they're not as vulnerable to daily fluctuations in currencies that can affect their bottom lines.

Currencies and Central Banks

Another key player in the foreign exchange market is the central banks of the world.

Central banks are responsible for the creation of currency in almost every country in the world. In the United States, this all-important regulator of monetary policy, the Federal Reserve Bank, commonly referred to as the Fed, is prominently newsworthy on a weekly, if not a daily, basis. Monetary policy is distinguished from fiscal policy, which is the domain of the president and Congress and is formulated through changes in taxes and government spending. The Fed's directors, appointed by the president and approved by the Senate, strive to maintain high employment, stable prices, and stable interest rates. The Fed exerts its authority primarily via monetary policy, such as lowering interest rates in order to promote economic growth and supplement employment opportunities. The rationale for this policy is easy to understand; if the economy needs stimulation, lowering interest rates should encourage business growth, thus easing unemployment.

The largest central banks operating in the world today are the Fed, which has existed since 1913; the European Central Bank, which has authority over the European Monetary Union, established in 1998; and the People's Bank of China, which has evolved into a more modern-looking central bank since 1989, when China developed a more capitalist-style export economy.

Central banks are also active players in the foreign exchange market. When currency fluctuations that are inconsistent with a nation's economic fundamentals are seen in the market, central banks can influence the value of their nations' currencies by intervening and buying or selling currencies. In fundamental terms, the rationale for such manipulation is that a central bank can raise or lower the value of its currency by buying or selling foreign currency in exchange for its own. Generally speaking, it is in the interest of governments to maintain a weak home currency. A weak, or less expensive, home currency boosts exports and economic growth, whereas a currency that is overly strong, or valuable, with respect to other currencies could hurt investment by raising the costs of the country's goods. Although this causal relationship is typically reliable, the economic repercussions of a strong or weak currency remain a subject of debate.

Central banks have also intervened in the foreign exchange market to manage currencies within political and economic alliances. In September of 1985, the G-5 finance ministers, representing the five leading economies of the day (the United States, the United Kingdom, Japan, Germany, and France), met at the Plaza Hotel in New York City and established the Plaza Accord, in which they agreed to collectively manipulate their currencies through foreign exchange transactions in order to devalue the U.S. dollar against the Japanese yen and the German deutsche mark. The goal was to restore the United States' competitive edge, as it had become the world's biggest debtor nation because of the amount of goods it imported, mostly produced in Japan, relative to the amount it exported. Many other measures were taken by the two governments because of this disparity, and U.S.-Japan relations were chilly for more than a decade as a result of this trade imbalance; however, the currency intervention was effective, with the yen doubling in value against the dollar in less than two years following the accord. Of course, this led to other problems, as Japan's economy then embarked on a downward slide.

The International Reserve System Today

The U.S. dollar has remained the world's reserve currency. In the most basic sense, this means that most major international transactions that involve the buying and selling of goods and services utilize U.S. dollars. When India sells goods to Brazil, for example, the Brazilian real gets converted to dollars to make the transaction. Historically, this came about because there were more U.S. dollars flooding the world than any other currency. On a related note, the U.S. dollar has also remained the world's safe haven currency. In times of economic stress, foreign governments buy U.S. Treasuries, as they feel that their money is safe if they invest it in U.S. government bonds, with the promise of yields, or interest paid on their investment over time; this phenomenon has persisted even when the rates for Treasuries have sunk to all-time lows in the summer of 2012.

An acute example of the safe haven appeal of the dollar was manifested in 2008, after the fall of Lehman Brothers, followed by the Great Recession. Currency traders unloaded holdings of foreign currencies around the globe and fled into what was perceived as the safety of the U.S. dollar. History has proven that the dominance of the dollar (being involved in fully 85 percent of the world's currency transactions), along with the depth and enormous liquidity of the U.S. Treasuries market, have made it the safest place to invest during times of panic and stress, even when the source of the economic unrest is attributable to events occurring in the United States. But the depth and severity of the financial crisis of 2008, compounded by a changing power dynamic in developed vs. emerging economies, are raising fundamental questions about how investors, central banks, and governments view the dollar—its value, its role, and its predominance.

CHAPTER 1

THE DOLLAR WILL REMAIN ON FIRST

G<small>ARY</small> S<small>HILLING</small>

"I just don't see at this point there is a major shift away from the dollar."
    —Ben Bernanke, *Federal Reserve Chairman, March 2011*

"Who's on first, What's on second, I Don't Know is on third," and so it goes in Abbott and Costello's marvelous routine that deliberately confuses baseball players' names with questions. In the game of global reserve currencies in future decades, we need to ask, Who's on first, Is Anyone on second, and Who Cares What's on third? By its nature, the currency roster always requires a batting order, since no currency operates independently in the international ballpark. The dollar doesn't stand alone, but against the euro, the yen, and even gold.

Reserve Currency Advantages

Of course, being the primary global reserve currency, the position enjoyed by the dollar since World War II, has tremendous advantages and creates a huge demand for greenbacks. Most of the world's trade is carried out in dollars, including trade and capital transactions that have no involvement with the United States. When Brazil sells iron ore to China, the transaction is probably in U.S. dollars. When Indians make a direct investment in Thailand, dollars are the likely medium of exchange.

Demand for bucks is supplied by foreign exchange reserves, which are mostly in dollars. Recently, foreigners' willingness, even zeal, to hold greenbacks has allowed and perhaps encouraged America to run chronic trade and current account deficits (Figure 1-1) because foreigners are happy to recycle the surplus dollars that result back into Treasuries and other U.S. investments.

Washington wizards figured out decades ago that if they're running a big budget deficit, they should also run a huge current

Figure 1-1   U.S. Current Account and Trade Balance

(Seasonally Adjusted Quarterly Data; $ in Billions)

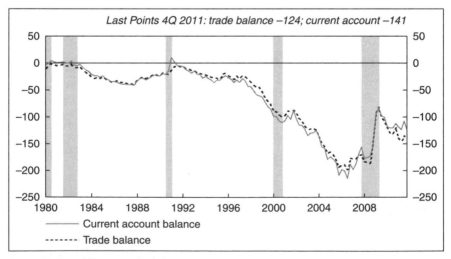

Source: Bureau of Economic Analysis

Figure 1-2 U.S. Personal Saving Rate

(Seasonally Adjusted Annual Rate)

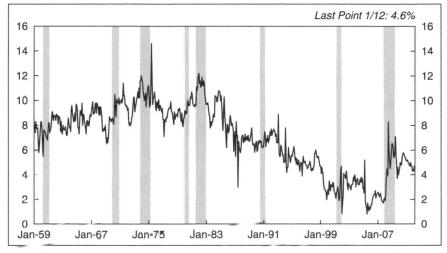

Source: Bureau of Economic Analysis

account deficit in order to get foreigners to pay for the federal red ink with dollars that are recycled into Treasuries. This game became more crucial as U.S. households slashed their saving rate for 25 years (Figure 1-2) and supplied less and less money to fund federal deficits and business investments, while hyping household borrowing (Figure 1-3).

$1 Trillion-Plus Deficits

Contrary to Congressional Budget Office projections, federal deficits in the $1 trillion-plus range are likely to persist if my forecast of chronic slow economic growth and chronic high unemployment is valid, and the resulting pressure on Washington to create jobs only increases. A key reason for the low 2 percent

Figure 1-3 Debt and Debt Service Payments as a Percentage of Disposable Personal Income

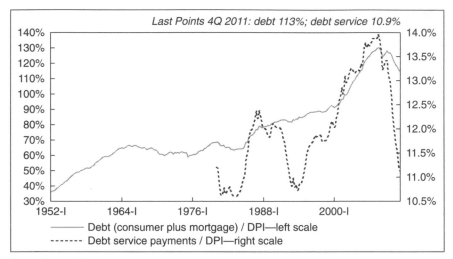

Last Points 4Q 2011: debt 113%; debt service 10.9%

——— Debt (consumer plus mortgage) / DPI—left scale
------ Debt service payments / DPI—right scale

Source: Federal Reserve

annual real GDP growth I forecast is my expectation that U.S. consumers will continue to deleverage, paying off the debts that they owe on their homes, credit cards, and other loans and pushing their saving rate back into double digits and the ratio of debt to disposable (after-tax) income back to its 65 percent norm.

This will compress the trade and current account deficits and reduce the amount of foreign-earned dollars that are recycled into federal deficit financing (assuming that foreigners continue to buy U.S. exports, since every 1 percent shortfall in consumer spending reduces our imports—the rest of the world's exports—by 2.8 percent). At the same time, however, more consumer saving will fund much more of the chronic high federal deficits. In the third quarter of 2011, disposable personal income was $11.6 trillion, so if the household saving rate were 10 percent, $1.16 trillion in consumer saving would be available to fund federal deficits and business investments.

Down Memory Lane

Let's take a stroll down memory lane to see what factors elevated various currencies to primary global trading and reserve status in the past. Not surprisingly, these currencies were linked to strong and sizable economies. The silver drachma issued in Athens in the fifth century BC was probably the first currency that circulated widely outside its issuer's borders, and it followed Alexander the Great (356–323 BC) as he conquered the then-known world from Egypt to Persia. Then, as Greece faded and Rome rose to global dominance, its gold aureus and silver denarius coins dominated, even though Athenian and Roman money circulated simultaneously for years.

But as the Roman Empire faded and the related inflation galloped, continually devalued Roman coins became less and less acceptable outside the empire. This and Rome's being overrun by Goths, Vandals, and Huns paved the way for the Byzantine Empire's gold solidus coin to become the standard for international trade in the sixth century.

In the seventh century, when the Arabs, flush with Muslim zeal, burst out of the Arabian Peninsula and charged across North Africa, the Arabian dinar partially replaced the solidus. The solidus was being debased to cover Byzantine deficits and was no longer solid, but it still circulated internationally into the eleventh century. Nevertheless, the Arabs also had government deficit problems and gradually devalued the dinar, starting at the end of the tenth century.

Florence and Venice

The merchants and bankers of Florence—the same guys who financed the Renaissance—began to flourish in the thirteenth century, and their currency, the fiorino, was used throughout the Mediterranean in commercial transactions. However, the Venetian ducato took over in the fifteenth century after Marco Polo (1253–1324) and others opened up the land route to China, and Venice became the western terminus of the Silk Road. Alas, the Portuguese then discovered the much easier water route to China around the southern tip of Africa, and Venice became the tourist trap it's been ever since while the ducato atrophied in international trade.

Global trade by water was the new technology of the seventeenth and eighteenth centuries, with the Dutch as the financial and commercial leaders, so the guilder reigned as the international currency. And paper money began to replace coins, even though it was not backed by the Dutch government. Spain, of course, controlled much of the New World after 1492, but the *real de a ocho*, or Spanish dollar, never really made the cut, since most of Spain's New World gold was dissipated in financing the Spanish Armada and other military disasters. In the nineteenth century, national central banks and treasuries began to hold gold as reserves, and bills and interest-bearing deposit claims that were gold substitutes also began to be held as reserves.

At the same time, the Industrial Revolution, which began in both England and New England in the late eighteenth century, made the United Kingdom the leading exporter of manufactured goods and services, and the biggest importer of food and industrial raw materials. As a result, sterling dominated as the international reserve and trading currency, and between the 1860s and the start of World War I in 1914, 60 percent of global trade was in pounds. With the advent of the telegraph and other communications advances, sterling was increasingly used in commercial transactions between non-U.K. residents. This role was also enhanced by London's emergence as the global leader in shipping and insurance and the center for both organized commodity markets and growing British foreign investments, usually denominated in sterling.

U.K. Sunset

Sterling's dominance in world trade started to slip before World War I, with the shares of the French franc, the German mark, and the U.S. dollar all increasing. Then World War I pretty much ended Britain's leading role in the international economy as economic interdependence broke down. Britain suspended the conversion of sterling into gold during the Great War, then reestablished it in 1925 at about prewar levels; this greatly overvalued sterling because of massive inflation in the meanwhile. With the Great Depression, the United Kingdom, the United States, and most other developed countries abandoned public conversion of paper currencies into gold.

With the rising power of the U.S. economy in global trade and finance, the dollar became the international currency starting in the 1920s, and it was crowned as the world's primary reserve currency by the Bretton Woods Agreement in 1944. The dollar was linked to gold, and all other currencies were linked to the dollar; this gave other countries access to the U.S. gold hoard, which had leaped during World War II, while fixing international exchange rates. But a foreign government rush for U.S. gold in the inflationary early 1970s forced President Nixon to sever the link to gold, and floating exchange rates for major economies followed.

The euro, introduced at the beginning of 1999, was heralded as a rival to the dollar as a reserve currency, reflecting the combined strength and size of the eurozone countries, which, together, had a GDP close to that of the United States. In the

Figure 1-4 U.S. Dollars per Euro

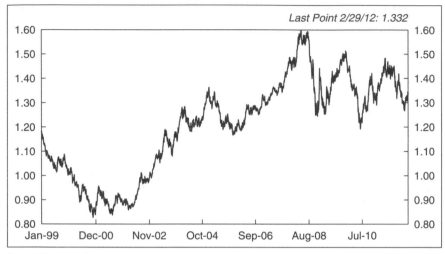

Source: Thomson Reuters

following decade, some countries moved a portion of their reserves to euros, and after an initial 30 percent drop from 1.18 euros per dollar to 0.83, the euro climbed steadily—until recent years (Figure 1-4).

The 2007–2009 Great Recession, however, revealed that joining the Teutonic north with the Club Med south under one currency but with no common fiscal policy was inherently flawed. It worked in the early to mid-2000s, when global economic growth covered up a multitude of sins, but not when tough times set in.

Eurozone Crisis

Germany and other strong countries in the Teutonic north have two unattractive options for dealing with the current crisis. They can continue, directly or through the European Central Bank, to bail out Greece and other weak countries, including potentially Spain and Italy. This strategy has no end in sight and is accompanied by rising resentment from their own voters. Or they can do nothing and wait for Greece to default on its sovereign debt, withdraw from the European Union (EU) and the eurozone, and devalue massively as it returns to drachmas, draculas, or whatever. Then there'd be a run on other Club Med country banks as investors yelled, "Who's next?," and contagion would force a disintegration of the eurozone as it is presently constituted.

That would bring big troubles for German, Dutch, and other strong country banks that have considerable exposure to the weak economies. So those countries' governments would have to bail out their own banks. As long as the crisis was confined to Greece, Ireland, and Portugal, it appeared manageable. Those three small countries combined account for less than 6 percent of eurozone GDP.

But if the woes spread to the other two PIIGS (PIIGS = Portugal, Ireland, Italy, Greece, and Spain), Spain and Italy, the problems will become huge whether the strong countries bail out the weak countries or their own banks. Spain accounted for 11.5 percent of eurozone GDP in the first quarter of 2012, and Italy accounted for 16.7 percent. All five of the PIIGS have high government deficits and debts. All except Ireland, which has given itself some very stringent fiscal medicine, have more and more risky sovereign debt issues, according to credit default swap prices. European banks that hold weak sovereign bonds are in trouble, and the woes of French banks and the French economy resulted in the January 2012 downgrade of French sovereign debt; Standard & Poor's also stripped Austria of its triple-A rating and reduced the ratings of Spain, Italy, and five other eurozone countries.

So the strong eurozone members need to bail out someone, and I think that they will continue to aid the weak countries directly. Otherwise, the eurozone will disintegrate, ending the noble post–World War II experiment in Europe. After the war, the German and French leaders decided that they had to find a different way of interacting from their method that had been used since Napoleon 150 years earlier—all-out war. They reasoned that integrating their economies more closely would reduce the likelihood of military conflict. That set them on the path that moved from the founding of the European Economic Community in 1958 to the eurozone in 1999. Complete political or even economic integration in such diverse countries was not feasible, but a common currency was believed to be an important step.

Sources of Strength

This review of history shows that primary reserve currencies are those that dominate international trade and are issued by robust economies. But how did these economies become robust? Alexander the Great knocked off every nation in sight by military conquest, including much, much larger Persia. Rome was notorious for conquering foreign lands and then carting the loot back to Rome. Egypt became the source of grain to provide the Roman multitudes with bread while Egyptian obelisks were moved to Rome as parts of the circuses.

Productivity Growth

In recent centuries, another element has superseded the grabbing of land and loot as a source of economic strength—productivity growth. In their 1988 book *American Business: A Two-Minute Warning* (New York: Free Press) C. Jackson Grayson, Jr., and Carla O'Dell make a very convincing case for superior productivity growth as the key to global economic leadership and, therefore, to principal reserve currency status. They explain that rapid productivity growth is necessary for raising living standards and achieving and maintaining global economic leadership.

They also note that earlier, the lack of productivity growth wasn't caused by a lack of technology. Ancient China, for example, was very technologically advanced, having invented gunpowder, umbrellas, movable type, paper making, and the magnetic compass. The strength of the Roman Empire, some argue, was the result of its advanced military technology. But ancient societies didn't apply their technologies to economic growth because they didn't want to upset the balance of power, vested interests, and stable societies.

No Growth

As a result, for millennia, world economic growth only kept up with population growth, and GDP per capita was static (Figure 1-5). According to Grayson and O'Dell, from 1500 to 1700, annual income rose from $215 per capita in current dollars to $265, a mere 0.1 percent per year. So it was a zero-sum world. Whatever Alexander or Rome gained, someone else lost.

But the Crusaders introduced Western Europeans to the East and its different cultures and products. Marco Polo and others developed the Silk Road to obtain spices, silks, and other things that were unknown in the West, and the desire to get to China by water led to the discovery of the New World. That not only shook up the old order but also gradually, very gradually, introduced conditions that promoted productivity and competition, not through arms but via commerce. And productivity became the means of raising living standards.

Figure 1-5 Growth in GDP per Capita

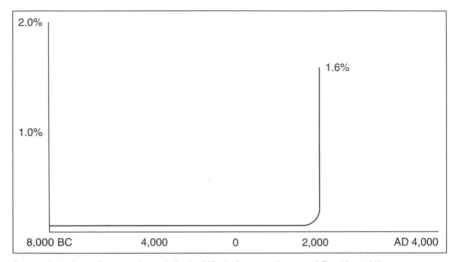

Source: C. Jackson Grayson, Jr., and Carla O'Dell, *American Business: A Two-Minute Warning* (New York: Free Press, 1988)

Now, let's be clear: productivity enhancement was not any nation's policy during the Age of Discovery or even in 1700, when it began to grow. Columbus got the backing of King Ferdinand and Queen Isabella to sail west to obtain gold and other riches, not to raise Spanish living standards. But the rise of towns in the Middle Ages and the circumnavigation of the globe worked to break down rigid controls and allowed Adam Smith's invisible hand, or the self-regulating nature of the free market, to get through the resulting crack in the door. With free markets, he argued, the pursuit of individuals' best interests increased the welfare and living standards of the whole community.

The Dutch

By 1700, global trading was the hot new technology, as mentioned earlier, and the Dutch were its masters from then until about 1785. They controlled not only the mouth of the Rhine, the water gateway to Europe, but also most of the trading routes to Southeast Asia. Grayson and O'Dell point out that in 1700, Dutch GDP per capita was about $440, or around 50 percent greater than England's $288. The Dutch had considerable expertise in producing woolens and linens, beer, ceramics, soap, and ships. Their fleet was bigger than England's, and, on a per capita basis, so was their international banking and insurance industry. Their low-cost textiles killed competitors in Genoa, Venice, and Milan.

The guilder was the international trading currency of the seventeenth and eighteenth centuries, as noted earlier. By the late 1700s, however, the Dutch got fat and happy and spent lots of time enjoying life and having their portraits painted by the successors to Rembrandt, van der Meer, and the boys. And they weren't carefully watching the ascendancy of the Brits.

Up until then, Dutch productivity exceeded that of England, but Holland's productivity growth slowed and even fell 0.1 percent annually during the latter part of the eighteenth century, according to Grayson and O'Dell. Meanwhile, English productivity growth accelerated to about 0.4 percent per year. The English gained on the Dutch in both agriculture and trade, and by 1760 they had overtaken the Netherlands to become the world's biggest trading nation.

U.K. Dominance

The United Kingdom's dominance really picked up steam with the unfolding there of the Industrial Revolution in the late 1700s. Among early inventions, the spinning jenny and the steam engine hyped productivity manyfold compared to hand spinning and weaving, and human and animal power. The Industrial Revolution, like any new technology, grew rapidly but started from zero, so it took decades before the effects on

British productivity were appreciable. Productivity in England rose only about 0.5 percent annually in the last several decades of the eighteenth century, but combined with stagnation in the Netherlands, British productivity surpassed that of the Dutch by about 1785.

The Industrial Revolution also had a profound effect on society. Think of the transformation from the days of Jane Austen's *Pride and Prejudice*, when jobs were beneath the dignity of the country gentry and prospective husbands were measured by their annual pensions from their families, to the wealth and power attained by the nineteenth-century industrialists and financiers, as exhibited by their "cottages" (mega-mansions) in Newport, Rhode Island.

The Middle Class

I've long believed that the greatest effect of the Industrial Revolution was to create vast middle classes. Earlier, European economies were two-class societies. Those on top owned almost everything and controlled most of the income. They spent lavishly on their palaces, entertainment, armies, and so forth, but they still had large saving rates. Those on the bottom spent all their income to subsist, but they had very little. Therefore, potential output was far in excess of domestic demand, and those countries tried to export it in return for gold. This, of course, was the strategy of the mercantilists, who held sway before the Industrial Revolution. But with the Industrial Revolution came the middle class, all those people who wanted a better life, conspicuous consumption, and education for their children. And they now had the money to pay for these desires. Hence the advent of domestic spending–led economies in developed countries—except in Japan, which clings to its feudalistic "export or die" mentality.

The rise of the middle class in Europe was reflected in the size of music halls. Earlier, classical music was composed for the nobles and church officials who were patrons of the musicians, and it was performed in rooms in their palaces—the chamber music of the Baroque and Classical periods. When J. S. Bach visited Frederick the Great at Potsdam in May 1747 and accepted the king's challenge to turn the 21 random notes that Frederick tapped out on a piano into his famous "Musical Offering," concerts, including flute concertos composed and performed by the king, in that magnificent palace were given in relatively small rooms with a dozen or so musicians.

In the nineteenth century, however, the rising middle class had money to spend on classical music, and musicians shifted to playing with large orchestras in huge concert halls to oblige these new patrons. Hector Berlioz went over the top in 1844 with a Paris concert that involved 1,022 performers, including 36 doubles basses for Beethoven's *Fifth Symphony*, 24 French horns for Weber's *Der Freischütz* overture, and 25 harps for Rossini's *Prayer of Moses*. In 1855, he followed with a spectacular performance featuring 1,200 players plus choruses and five subconductors.

Nineteenth-Century England

With Britain being the first major country to industrialize and its resulting 1.5 percent annual productivity growth between 1820 and 1870, it dominated the nineteenth century in manufacturing, global trade, and finance, and in political and military power after Napoleon met his Waterloo in 1815, despite the United Kingdom's relatively small land mass and population. In 1870, according to Grayson and O'Dell, Britain's trade was greater than that of France, Germany, and Italy combined and three times that of the United States. And, as noted earlier, sterling dominated in international trade and was the world's reserve currency, and the sun never set on the British Empire that stretched across the globe.

But like the Dutch before them, the British became complacent in the late 1800s and let their productivity growth slip below that of two upstarts—Germany and the United States. Probably because of its physical proximity and differences in culture and language, the threat from Germany was expressed more frequently in the British press, Parliament, and business community. A Royal Commission in 1885 found that in the production of goods, Britain had few, if any, advantages over Germany and that the Germans "appeared to be gaining ground on British business."

Nevertheless, the two world wars in the first half of the twentieth century knocked Germany out of the box, at least temporarily. And with the American Industrial Revolution in full flower in the late 1800s and railroads spreading across the continent, the United States became the major challenge to Britain.

As noted earlier, the Industrial Revolution in America commenced in New England in the late 1700s, at the same time as its genesis in England, but it came into full flower and became big enough to drive the economy only after the Civil War. Agricultural value added was almost twice that of manufacturing at the beginning of that conflict (Figure 1-6), but the explosion of factory output equalized the shares of the two by the mid-1880s. At the end of the century, factories outproduced farms by almost two to one. Between 1860 and 1914, employment in manufacturing and construction tripled, and the physical output of manufacturing rose six times.

Figure 1-6 Value Added in U.S. Commodity Output by Sectors, 1859–1899

	Agriculture	Manufacturing	Mining	Construction
1859	56	32	1	11
1869	53	33	2	12
1874	40	39	2	12
1879	49	37	3	11
1884	41	44	3	12
1889	37	48	4	11
1894	32	53	4	11
1899	33	53	5	9

Source. Robert E. Gallman, *Trends in the American Economy in the Nineteenth Century,* Conference on Research in Income and Weatlh, (Princeton, NJ: Princeton University Press, 1960)

Railroads

Railroads were first developed in England in the mid-1700s, but only after the Civil War did this new technology become big enough to drive the U.S. economy. Railroads pushed across the continent, uniting first North and South, then East and West. In 1860, the United States had 30,626 miles of track, mostly in the East, Midwest, and South; by 1900, the United States had 198,964 miles of track. Trains crisscrossing the nation carried people westward and brought agricultural products and minerals east, thus opening up vast acreage for farmers, ranchers, and miners.

More Productivity

Overall, U.S. productivity after the Civil War grew at a sustained rate unequaled during any other period in history. Real GNP per capita grew at an average annual rate of 2.1 percent from 1869 to 1898, and the population grew at about the same rate, encouraged by waves of immigrants. Consequently, real GNP grew 4.3 percent per year in the greatest period of sustained growth in American history. That compares with 3.7 percent in the unsustainable salad years of 1982 to 2000.

Notice, in comparison, the much slower growth in the United Kingdom and France during the latter part of the nineteenth and early twentieth centuries (Figure 1-7). Without meaningful immigration, population growth was much slower than that in the United States, and the Industrial Revolution bloom was off the rose, especially in the pioneer industrialist nation, the United Kingdom. Canada, naturally, resembled the United States.

After Bismarck assembled the various German states into one nation and industrialization commenced, the country's growth was strong, but the immigrant population growth of the United States was missing. The same was true of Japan

Figure 1-7 Growth by Country, 1869–1914

	Period	GNP	GNP per Capita	Population
United States	1869–1878 to 1904–1913	56.0%	27.5%	22.3%
United Kingdom	1860–1869 to 1905–1914	25.0%	12.5%	11.1%
France	1841–1850 to 1901–1910	18.6%	16.3%	1.9%
Germany	1860–1869 to 1905–1914	35.6%	21.6%	11.5%
Canada	1870–1879 to 1905–1914	47.1%	24.7%	17.8%
Japan	1878–1887 to 1903–1912	49.2%	33.7%	11.6%

Source: S. S. Kuznets, Economic Development and Social Change (October, 1956)

after Commodore Perry's show of American naval and industrial firepower in 1854 convinced the leaders there that feudalism had to go in favor of industrialization.

U.S. Ascendancy

In 1870, the U.S. productivity level was fourth, behind not only England, the leader, but also the Netherlands and Belgium (Figure 1-8). However, the United States overtook Holland in the 1870s and Belgium in the 1880s, and then bested the United Kingdom. American productivity growth averaged 2.1 percent per year from 1870 to 1890, far exceeding the United Kingdom's 1.3 percent rate. As that 0.8 percent gap compounded, American productivity levels spurted beyond those of Britain in the 1890s. Not surprisingly, by 1901, U.S. per capita GDP exceeded that of the United Kingdom.

Many people believe that it was the disaster of World War I that knocked the United Kingdom off the throne, but it had actually occurred 13 years before the war started, and the seeds had been sown 45 years before that, when U.S. productivity growth leaped above that of Britain. Think about it! America,

Figure 1-8   1870 Productivity Levels

England = 100

England	100
Netherlands	93
Belgium	93
United States	88
Germany (7th)	54

Source: C. Jackson Grayson, Jr., and Carla O'Dell, *American Business: A Two-Minute Warning* (New York: Free Press, 1988)

a mere colony through most of the eighteenth century, then a thorn in the side of mighty Britain in the late eighteenth and early nineteenth centuries, overtook the mother country at the beginning of the twentieth century and has been in the lead ever since. It's not surprising, then, that the dollar replaced the pound sterling as the world's reserve currency after World War II.

Nevertheless, currencies that other countries hold as part of their national treasuries die hard—they hate to desert old friends—so sterling did not begin to fall against the dollar until World War I, and it remained in some countries' official reserves until well beyond World War II. We've been told that in the Golden Triangle, the area where Thailand, Burma, and Laos meet and the drug trade thrives, British gold sovereign coins were the medium of exchange in the 1990s, a century after they were minted. Do they still circulate?

On the eve of World War I, U.S. productivity was 25 percent higher than that in the United Kingdom, and it was 42 percent higher at the beginning of World War II. And it grew tremendously during the war as a result of new technology, flexibility of the labor force, with women working (remember Rosie the Riveter, the housewife who worked in a defense plant to replace men in the military?), and cooperation among markets, labor, and government under the threat of wartime conditions. Since America was the only major country whose productive capacity was not decimated by the war, European productivity was only 30 to 40 percent and Japan's a mere 14 percent of the U.S. level after the war.

Military Might

Some people note that countries with international trading and reserve currencies are those with a dominant military.

That's been true historically, from ancient Greece and Rome to Byzantium, to Venice, with its forts that controlled the sea route from the Adriatic to the Middle East, to Britain in the nineteenth century, to the United States since then. But is there a distinct causal relationship?

At least since ancient times, military power didn't create international currencies. Rather, robust productivity growth and high levels of output per worker created the economic strength that allowed countries to divert considerable resources to military spending. That was probably true of Venice in its heyday, and it was clearly true of Britain in the nineteenth century, despite the slogan, "Trade follows the flag." It more correctly should have been, "Trade expansion promotes the flag." In the last century, a robust, productivity-led U.S. economy was necessary to support sizable defense outlays, especially in the post–World War II era of the Cold War, the Korean and Vietnam Wars, and, more recently, involvement in Iraq and Afghanistan. Without such an economy, voters in our democracy would probably have rebelled when their purchasing power was squeezed to support a huge military establishment.

Ingredients for a Successful International Currency

This review of both history and modern reality reveals six necessary ingredients for a dominant international trade and reserve currency.

1. *Rapid growth in the economy and GDP per capita, promoted by robust productivity growth.* This is probably the most necessary condition for a dominant international trade and reserve currency. It was the key to British sterling's

success in the nineteenth century and the dollar's superior position since then. It's also necessary to support globally dominant military structures in modern democracies while still satisfying voters by providing them with acceptable standards of living.

2. *A large economy, probably the world's biggest.* That was true of ancient Rome, which had an unusually effective administration and centralized control for the times. With the breakdown of communications in the Middle Ages, size became less important, allowing relatively small Italian city-states and their currencies to achieve international primacy. In modern times, Singapore and Switzerland meet my other qualifications but are just not big enough to have primary currencies.

3. *Deep and broad financial markets.* Internationally, money—especially today, when it can be transferred anywhere in a split second—wants to be where the action is. That requires not only a powerful and large economy, but also deep and broad markets in which to invest. Today, the U.S. Treasury market trumps all others in size and, in the eyes of investors (Figure 1-9), in safety, as witnessed by the mad rush into Treasury bonds in the ongoing European sovereign debt crisis. Similarly, America has the largest stock market by far (Figure 1-10).

4. *Free and open financial markets and economy.* Foreign investors are willing to hold a country's currency only if they are convinced that they can invest it in financial or tangible assets in that country with few restrictions. The United States is essentially open, which is necessary if the Chinese and Japanese are to continue to recycle their current account surpluses with the United States into Treasuries and other American investments.

Figure 1-9   2010 G-7 and Eurozone Net Debt Outstanding

($ in Billions)

United States	9,928
Eurozone	8,022*
Japan	6,400
PIIGS total	3,163
Italy	2,042
France	1,962
Germany	1,892
United Kingdom	1,523
Spain	518
Canada	508
Greece	329
Portugal	153
Ireland	122
* Does not include Cyprus, Luxembourg, Malta, Slovakia, or Slovenia.	

Source: International Monetary Fund

Figure 1-10   Equity Market Capitalization

($ in Trillions)

United States (Nasdaq and NYSE)	14.045
Eurozone*	4.760
China (Shenzen and Shanghai)	3.627
Japan (Tokyo Stock Exchange)	3.453
United Kingdom (London)	3.105
* Consists of Deutsche Borse, NYSE Euronext (Europe), BME Spanish Exchanges, Irish Stock Exchange, Athens Exchange, Luxembourg Stock Exchange, and Malta Stock Exchange.	

Source: World Federation of Exchanges

5. *Lack of substitutes.* A primary global currency, by definition, has no close competitors. The risk is that the top dog gets fat and lazy while upstarts surpass it in productivity growth, and ultimately in GDP per capita or GDP per employee. That's how the Dutch lost out to the British in the late 1700s and, in turn, the United Kingdom was overrun by the United States a little more than a century later.

6. *Credibility in the value of the currency.* Internationally, money is fleet-footed, is congenitally cautious, and runs from uncertainty over risk of confiscation, debasement, and other threats, as discussed in our earlier review of history. The Roman aureus, the Byzantine solidus, and the Arabian dinar all went out of international style when those empires waned, but the related debasement of those currencies speeded the exit. On the flip side, in World War I, Britain went off the gold standard, only to return in 1925 with the prewar price of gold in sterling. Given the immense wartime inflation in the interim, that action vastly overpriced the sterling, causing uncertainty and leading to a mass exodus of U.K. money to New York and elsewhere.

Is a Reserve Currency Needed?

Of course, my six criteria for a primary international trade and reserve currency raise the question of whether one is needed at all. And if it is, can two exist simultaneously?

Advantages of Gold

It's hard to envision today's global business without some international standard. Likewise, it seems unlikely that major governments would be satisfied with only their own domestic

Figure 1-11 Gold Prices and CPI (Consumer Price Index)

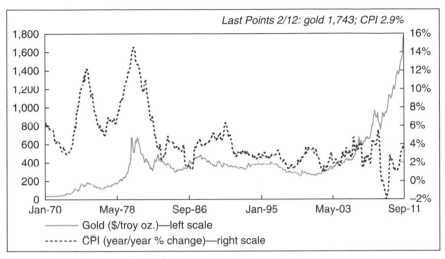

Last Points 2/12: gold 1,743; CPI 2.9%

——— Gold ($/troy oz.)—left scale

------ CPI (year/year % change)—right scale

Source: Kitco and Bureau of Labor Statistics

assets, financial or tangible, as reserves. Some people believe that the international standard and reserve asset should be gold, and its price explosion in recent years, at least until recently, suggests a disdain for all paper currencies (Figure 1-11). Gold doesn't oxidize, and the total supply today is relatively stable, since new mine production is tiny compared to what has been refined and retained over the ages.

This is quite different from the period when the gigantic inflow of gold from the New World in the 1500s created huge inflation in Europe after centuries of price stability (Figure 1-12). Also working to keep supply stable, gold, unlike silver, has few industrial uses, although the BBC and other news media reported that Col. Gadhafi was shot and killed by an eighteen-year-old wearing a New York Yankees baseball cap using the colonel's gold-plated pistol! And given the traditional French love of gold, French bank chieftains must wish they owned gold rather than the PIIGS sovereign issues that threaten to sink them.

Figure 1-12 U.K. Retail Price Index

(1264 = 100)

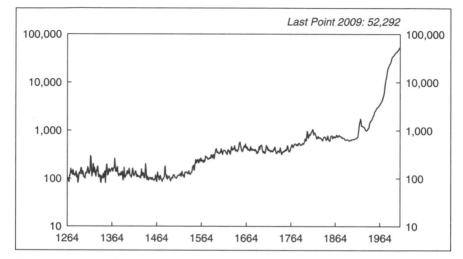

Source: measuringworth.com

I've always been agnostic on the price of gold. It's difficult for me to sort out all the forces involved—buying and selling by central banks, new mining techniques, political and inflation/deflation fears, the Indians who buy gold when they're rich and trade it for silver when they're not, the actions of gold bugs, and so on. It seems that when one of these forces dominates, as did inflation fears in the late 1970s (Figure 1-11) and probably flight from all fiat currencies (paper currencies, or money with no inherent value other than the denomination printed on it) recently, gold prices react. But with disinflation starting in the early 1980s, gold prices fell for 20 years by 61 percent nominally and 83 percent in real terms as negative factors affecting its price overcame positive influences.

Drawbacks of Gold

Gold has a number of drawbacks as an international trading and reserve currency. Its price in early 2012 climbed to $1,656 per troy ounce, but it would need to leap to $8,158 just to replace the broad money supplies in the United States, Canada, Japan, the United Kingdom, and the eurozone, even if all the refined gold in the world were employed, with none left for jewelry or to plate Col. Gadhafi's pistol. It's expensive to store, and it has no return unless it's lent out. It's also heavy to carry around and at high risk of theft. Recall all those gold-laden Spanish galleons that were either captured by English buccaneers or sunk in the Caribbean, waiting four centuries or more for treasure hunters to find them.

Of course, gold could be deposited safely and paper certificates issued against it. Ancient Chinese paper currency was backed by and denominated in strings of coins. U.S. dollar bills used to be silver certificates backed by Treasury silver holdings. But as was shown in ancient China, once paper is issued, it's hard to limit its linkage to metal to strict amounts. So you're pretty much back to the current system where the tie of paper currencies to anything else is tenuous at best.

Furthermore, if gold is the only money and any paper issued against it is strictly limited, governments have no monetary control. William Jennings Bryan, in his "Cross of Gold" speech that helped him win the Democratic presidential nomination in 1896, argued for the free coinage of silver to break the gold monopoly of the money supply. Western farmers and ranchers who wanted plenty of money and cheap credit to expand were pitted against eastern bankers who liked high returns on their loans. Well, Bryan lost to William McKinley, who was assassinated and succeeded by Theodore Roosevelt. Go figure.

Figure 1-13   Gold Prices

(Dollars per Troy Ounce; Nearest Futures Contract)

Source: Thomson Reuters

In 1971, President Nixon was forced to sever the dollar's link to gold when a run on the yellow metal threatened to exhaust U.S. gold reserves, as noted earlier. The recent run-up and then nosedive in gold's price (Figure 1-13) suggests that it continues to be subject to rallies and retreats, at least in relation to the dollar. And the system could be thrown into chaos if huge new sources of gold were discovered, comparable to the New World finds in the 1500s.

If gold were money and any paper currency issued against it were strictly limited, what would occupy central bankers? Like the individual eurozone banks since the advent of the ECB, whose mandate does not allow them to print money, would they essentially spend their days counting coins and bills? Conventional monetary policies, that is, raising and lowering interest-rate targets to either fight inflation or stimulate economic growth, would still be possible, but if interest rates got to zero, as at present, central banks would be impotent. Quantitative easing, which injects more money into the economy by purchasing financial assets, would be out, since central banks could no longer create money out of thin air. (Of course, the Ron Pauls of the world, who want to abolish central banks—and perhaps some other antagonists of Fed Chairman Bernanke as well— would probably be happy to see this state of affairs.)

Two vs. One?

These problems with gold suggest that despite the current concerns over the dollar and other fiat currencies, gold is unlikely to become the primary global trade currency and reserve asset. But could two international currencies exist simultaneously? Until the eurozone sovereign debt crisis erupted in 2010 and a hard landing in China became more widely expected, many observers saw the dollar losing its primacy to the ascending euro and, later, the Chinese yuan. Some Middle East oil producers shifted meaningful amounts of reserves into euros.

In the seventh century, both the Byzantine solidus and the Arabian dinar circulated internationally, although the solidus was on the way out along with Byzantium, while the dinar was ascending in line with Arab conquests. Similarly, both sterling and the U.S. dollar were international reserve currencies in the early 1900s, when the United States was rising in global power and the United Kingdom was slipping. In both cases, dual international currencies existed not in periods of stability but during the transition from one to the other.

The expected rise in the euro as a currency in wide use outside the eurozone was probably responsible, at least in part, for the weakness in the dollar in the 2000s (Figure 1-14). But the

Figure 1-14 U.S. Dollar Index

(Vs. Major Currencies)

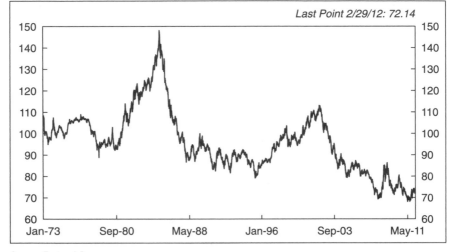

Source: Federal Reserve

eurozone crisis has cut off the ascendancy of the euro, and those Middle Eastern countries have apparently moved their reserves back to dollars.

The Dollar's Scoreboard

Is the dollar likely to remain the world's primary international trade and reserve currency in coming decades? To see, let's examine the greenback against my six criteria for this status.

Productivity Growth

In the last decade, productivity growth was rapid in countries like Estonia, Poland, Hungary, the Czech Republic, and Slovakia, which have been catching up as they shake off the last vestiges of Soviet repression (Figure 1-15). South Korea's productivity

Figure 1-15 Productivity Growth

(2000–2010 Calculated Annual Growth Rate)

Estonia	4.8%
Slovakia	4.5%
Korea	4.3%
Russia	4.2%
Turkey	3.7%
Czech Republic	3.5%
Poland	3.2%
Hungary	2.9%
Iceland	2.6%
Chile	2.6%
Slovenia	2.6%
United States	2.2%
Ireland	2.0%
Sweden	1.6%
Japan	1.6%
Greece	1.5%
Finland	1.5%
Australia	1.3%
Israel	1.2%
Austria	1.2%
Netherlands	1.2%
United Kingdom	1.2%
Portugal	1.1%
Spain	1.1%
New Zealand	1.1%
Germany	0.9%
Canada	0.9%
Switzerland	0.8%
France	0.8%
Norway	0.7%
Denmark	0.6%
Belgium	0.5%
Mexico	0.3%
Luxembourg	0.2%
Italy	0.0%
Eurozone	0.8%
G-7	1.6%
OECD total	1.6%

Source: Organisation for Economic Co-operation and Development

growth, 4.3 percent per year in the 2000–2010 decade, was rapid, but as the country becomes more and more a developed country, it is less and less able to grow rapidly by emulating the leaders. Indeed, annual South Korean productivity growth has dropped consistently from 7.9 percent in 1985–1990 to 4.4 percent in 2005–2010. Unfortunately, reliable data for China are not available, but its productivity growth is probably slowing as opportunities to acquire Western technology play out.

Among developed countries, the United States, with 2.2 percent annual productivity growth in the last decade, was clearly the leader. Japan struggled at 1.6 percent per year. The United Kingdom was even lower, 1.2 percent. The countries in the eurozone ranged from zero in Italy to 2.0 percent in Ireland, and averaged 0.8 percent. Notice that the other PIIGS benefited from the euro, with Greek productivity gaining 1.5 percent per year, Portuguese 1.1 percent, and Spanish 1.1 percent, but those numbers will be hard to sustain in the aftermath of the current eurozone sovereign debt crisis. In contrast, annual productivity growth was only 0.9 percent in stalwart Germany and 0.8 percent in France.

The *level* of productivity, measured by GDP per hour worked, is also the highest in the United States, $59.5, with few exceptions (Figure 1-16). Luxembourg is concentrated in banking and other high-value-added industries, Norway has a small population and big petroleum revenues, and the Netherlands has a well-educated and homogenous population. But beyond that, even the hardworking Germans had lower GDP per hour worked in 2010 than the United States, $53.4, and when the less-diligent Club Med countries are included, the Eurozone as a whole was much lower, $49.1. The United Kingdom ran $46.7, and, surprisingly, the dedicated Japanese produced only $39.4 in GDP per hour worked

Figure 1-16   2010 Productivity

	GDP per Head of Population (US$)	GDP per Hour Worked, Current Prices (US$)
Luxembourg	89,633	70.5
Norway	56,648	75.4
Netherlands	42,478	59.6
United States	47,425	59.5
Belgium	37,435	58.8
Ireland	39,778	57.9
France	33,835	54.8
Germany	37,567	53.4
Denmark	39,545	50.8
Sweden	39,013	49.8
Austria	39,768	49.4
Switzerland	46,390	48.5
Spain	32,070	47.4
Finland	36,664	47.3
Australia	39,406	46.9
United Kingdom	35,917	46.7
Canada	38,891	45.0
Italy	31,563	43.5
Japan	33,737	39.4
Iceland	34,747	39.2
Slovenia	27,545	35.7
Israel	29,211	35.4
New Zealand	29,803	33.9
Slovakia	23,448	33.8
Greece	28,189	32.4
Portugal	25,609	32.2
Korea	29,004	27.1
Czech Republic	25,299	26.9
Estonia	20,608	26.7
Hungary	20,325	25.9
Turkey	15,522	25.8
Poland	19,747	24.5
Russia	19,819	20.5
Mexico	15,204	19.8
Chile	15,061	19.2
G-7	40,114	51.7
Eurozone	34,292	49.1
OECD 30	34,430	44.3
OECD total	34,103	43.9

Source: Organisation for Economic Co-operation and Development

in 2010. But then the Japanese economy remains a combination of a highly efficient export sector and an inefficient domestic component.

Normal and Fast

Furthermore, the recent productivity growth rate in the United States is normal. Annual nonfarm business-sector productivity, averaged by decades, has been between 2 percent and 2.5 percent since 1900 (Figure 1-17). Even in the 1930s Great Depression, it averaged 2.4 percent as the new technologies of the 1920s, such as the electrification of homes and factories, telephones, and mass-produced autos, continued to gain importance, even in the flagging economy.

The exception was in the 1970s and 1980s, when first Vietnam disrupted the economy, and then the inflation spawned by huge Great Society spending on top of oversized military outlays led

Figure 1-17   Productivity in the U.S. Nonfarm Business Sector

(Average Annual Growth Rate by Decade)

	NBER	BLS
1901–1910	2.34%	NA
1911–1920	2.64%	NA
1921–1930	2.07%	NA
1931–1940	2.39%	NA
1941–1950	2.46%	NA
1951–1960	2.28%	2.14%
1961–1970	2.49%	2.71%
1971–1980	NA	1.45%
1981–1990	NA	1.61%
1991–2000	NA	2.18%
2001–2010	NA	2.36%

Sources: National Bureau of Economic Research (NBER); Bureau of Labor Statistics (BLS)

to serious price increases. Respect for authority virtually disappeared, and the postwar babies entered the workforce as undisciplined, raw recruits. Since then, of course, U.S. productivity growth has returned to its century-old trend.

American productivity growth will probably remain robust in the decades ahead. For nine distinct reasons (Figure 1-18), I expect slow U.S. economic growth in future years, averaging 2 percent annually for real GDP. This compares with the post–World War II average of 3.2 percent and the rapid 3.7 percent rate in the 1982–2000 salad days, when inflation was unwinding and American consumers were on a borrowing and spending binge. In the ongoing environment of slow corporate revenue growth, businesses will no doubt continue to promote productivity and otherwise cut costs. The recent surge in temporary employment should continue, since those people work only at the time of day or season of the year that

Figure 1-18 Nine Causes of Slow Global Growth in Future Years

1. U.S. consumers will shift from a 25-year borrowing and-spending binge to a saving spree. This will spread abroad as American consumers curtail the imports of the goods and services that many foreign nations depend on for economic growth.

2. Financial deleveraging will reverse the trend that financed much global growth in recent years.

3. Increased government regulation and involvement in major economies will stifle innovation and reduce efficiency.

4. Low commodity prices will limit spending by commodity-producing lands.

5. Developed countries are moving toward fiscal restraint.

6. Rising protectionism will slow—or even eliminate—global growth.

7. The housing market will be weak because of excess inventories and loss of investment appeal.

8. Deflation will curtail spending as buyers anticipate lower prices.

9. State and local governments will contract.

they're needed, and their benefits tend to be much lower than those of full-time workers.

Also reflecting the new trend is the rise in job openings while new hires remain flat. With high unemployment providing an ample supply of job candidates and amidst continuing layoffs, businesses are picky and insist on highly productive new employees who are well trained, educated, and experienced.

Furthermore, the United States, with many top universities and a robust entrepreneurial culture, is likely to continue to lead the world in productivity-soaked new technologies such as semiconductors, computers, the Internet, telecom, and biotech. As in any technology-driven growth binge, these technologies aren't all that new. Computers have been around since World War II; semiconductors were invented in 1947; and the first PCs, Commodore and Apple II, appeared in 1977. But only now are they and the huge amount of productivity that they enable becoming big enough to drive the economy. Apple started as a computer for techies but leaped to major economic influence years later with the iPod, the iPhone, and then the iPad.

Economic Size

Economic size will also favor the United States for many years. In the second quarter of 2010, China surpassed Japan to become the world's second largest economy (Figure 1-19), but its GDP was still only 40 percent of America's in 2010. Because China has 1.338 billion people, or 4.3 times as many as America, the per capita GDP gap was even bigger. China's $4,393 was only 9 percent of the $47,184 in the United States.

These differences mean that China has to grow very rapidly in future years, much faster than the United States, just to maintain these gaps, let alone close them. I assume that U.S.

Figure 1-19   2010 GDP, Population, and GDP per Capita

	$ Billion	% of United States	Population (million)	GDP per Capita ($)
United States	14,582.4	100.0%	309.1	47,184
Eurozone	12,174.5	83.5%	331.7	36,706
China	5,878.6	40.3%	1,338.3	4,393
Japan	5,497.8	37.7%	127.5	43,137
United Kingdom	2,246.1	15.4%	62.2	36,100
India	1,729.0	11.9%	1,170.9	1,477

Source: World Bank

real GDP rises 2.0 percent per year on average for the next decade, but let's extend that for 30 years. Government projections have the U.S. population rising to 402 million in 2039, or about 1 percent per year, as continuing immigration offsets subreplacement-level fertility rates. The Chinese population is expected to rise to 1.395 billion in 2026, but then fall to 1.363 billion in 2039 as its one-child-per-family policy reduces total population.

To just maintain the per capita GDP gap between the United States and China at $42,791 in 2010 dollars, Chinese GDP growth will need to continue at double-digit rates for four years before tapering off, or rise six times in three decades one way or the other. Furthermore, to close the per capita GDP gap in 30 years, Chinese GDP would need to grow about 10 percent per year for three decades, or expand 17.8 times in that period. Wow!

Limits to Chinese Growth

China is highly unlikely to continue its double-digit economic growth for many more years. It's relatively easy for developing countries to grow rapidly by emulating the technology of the leaders or, in China's case, forcing them to share it as the price of doing business in China. Furthermore, many Chinese firms have no qualms about stealing Western technology and intellectual property. But as those lands approach developed country status, rapid productivity growth falters, and they must develop cutting-edge technology themselves. China's reliance on exports and a controlled currency for growth will no longer work if U.S. consumers are engaged in a chronic saving spree, as I forecast. Average Chinese export growth of 21 percent per year on average in the last decade is bound to suffer.

China's seemingly inexhaustible pool of cheap labor is expected to peak in 2014 (Figure 1-20), in part because of the country's rigid one-child-per-couple policy. Young people are the ones who are most willing to relocate for work, and those folks are already declining in number, with 15- to 24-year-olds

Figure 1-20 Chinese Working-Age Population

(Millions of 15- to 65-Year-Olds)

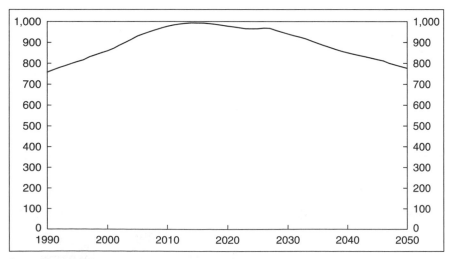

Source: Census Bureau

falling from 250 million in 1990 to a projected 150 million by 2030. Estimates are that an ample supply of labor has boosted GDP growth by 1.8 percentage points annually since the late 1970s, but the contraction of the working-age population will reduce growth by 0.7 percentage point by 2030, a 2.5-percentage-point swing.

Wages are already rising in China, and some Chinese manufacturers are moving production to Vietnam and Pakistan, where pay levels are a third of China's. Wage increases of 20 to 30 percent have been seen in the last year or so, especially for factory workers producing goods for foreign companies. At the same time, better conditions in rural areas have cut the availability of cheap labor in coastal cities, as fewer people move there from the hinterland. Rural wages, which largely reflect the pay of migrant workers in factories and at construction sites, have risen 15 percent in real terms in the past year. Minimum-wage increases throughout Chinese provinces averaged 23 percent in 2010. Beijing favors higher wages, despite the negative effect on exports, in order to push up consumer incomes and spending in its zeal for a more domestically driven economy.

As the Chinese population ages, the ratio of retirees to working-age people is forecast to rise from 39 percent last year to 46 percent in 2025. Note, however, that at the same time, the ratio in Japan will rise from an already elevated 56 percent to 69 percent and that in the United States from 50 percent to 58 percent. Still, Japan and the United States have a lot more income and resources per capita to support retirees than does China.

Planned Changes

Chinese leaders seem to be well aware that the 2007–2009 global recession and financial crisis was a wake-up call and that they need to change their economic orientation. In October 2010, the Communist Party leadership conference called for "accelerating the transformation of the nation's economic development pattern" and "putting more emphasis on securing and improving people's livelihood to promote social equality and justice."

The new Five-Year Plan calls for lower export growth, around 10 percent per year, compared to the 24 percent average in the five years before the global recession and financial crisis. It also increases the share of labor income in GDP, which fell from 57 percent to 50 percent between 1997 and 2007 while corporate profits and government revenue shares grew, as well as consumption's share of GDP, which dropped from 45 percent to 34 percent since 2001 (Figure 1-21). China is clearly the outlier in terms of consumption's share of GDP. In 2010, this

Figure 1-21 Chinese Consumption, Exports, and Investment as a Percentage of GDP

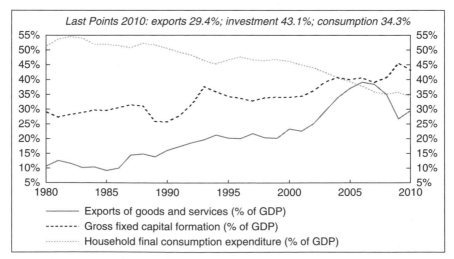

Source: World Bank

share was 48 percent in Russia, 58 percent in Brazil and Germany, 59 percent in Japan, 63 percent in India, 66 percent in the United Kingdom, and 71 percent in free-spending America.

Big Savers

A key reason that Chinese spending is subdued is that households are such big savers (Figure 1-22). Even with their limited income, they save close to 30 percent of it, on average. They save because in a Confucian culture, people feel responsible for providing for their families. They also save a lot to cover unemployment, old age and medical costs, job insecurity risks, and their children's education. When the Communist leaders moved the economy from a cradle-to-grave nanny state to a progressively free-market orientation beginning in 1978, and the "iron rice bowl" disappeared, no meaningful unemployment,

Figure 1-22   Chinese Household Saving Rate

(Annual Average)

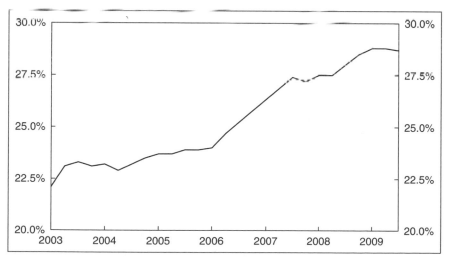

Source: Chinese National Bureau of Statistics

government retirement, or health systems were instituted to replace the dismantled government programs, free education, free housing, and lifetime job guarantees. The Chinese government is planning to institute retirement and healthcare plans, and President Hu said in October 2010 that it will "institute a social safety net that covers all." But it probably will do so gradually. The government in 2009 set a goal of providing basic medical care for all Chinese by 2020 at the cost of $125 billion. But that's eight years away, and in China, basic medical care is very basic!

The Chinese saving rate will also be pushed down in time by aging Chinese who still consume but no longer work, much as in Japan. Nevertheless, lower saving and more Chinese consumption won't substitute for weakening exports any time soon. Chinese consumers spend only about one-tenth of what those in Europe and the United States combined spend. As the eurozone remains troubled, the United Kingdom slashes government stimuli, and U.S. consumers continue to retrench, it's unlikely that a drop in Chinese saving and the resulting rise in consumer spending could offset the Western countries' negative effects on Chinese exports.

Fertility

The U.S. fertility rate, the highest among the G-7 countries (Figure 1-23), will also aid its dominance in economic size. Meanwhile, China's one-child-per-family policy implies a declining population. Japan's population is already declining because of its low fertility rates and strict limits on immigration.

Japan continues to be the least friendly to immigrants of any major country, so it lacks a meaningful influx of people from abroad. There's no such thing as an immigration visa, although foreigners have been allowed in during times of labor shortages

Figure 1-23 G-7 Fertility Rates

(2011 Estimates)

United States	2.06
France	1.96
United Kingdom	1.91
Canada	1.58
Germany	1.41
Italy	1.39
Japan	1.21

Source: CIA World Factbook

for extended "training sessions." As I understand it, baseball is not a native Japanese sport, but, like golf, was the result of emulation of Yankees during the American occupation after World War II. Yet Japanese baseball teams are allowed no more than three foreigners. Another factor dragging down future economic growth, is that the number of older Japanese is growing much faster than their counterparts elsewhere, and the Japanese have the highest life expectancy of any developed country (Figure 1-24).

In contrast, the United States is a nation of immigrants and has been since the first Europeans arrived 500 years ago. As a result, it has always been a relatively easy country to get into and stay in, despite the recent flap over illegal aliens. Once legal or illegal immigrants are here, they can disappear into the population indefinitely. That's far different from the situation in Europe, where the cheerful hotel check-in clerk who asks for your passport is sending your whereabouts directly to the local police. Young immigrants, many of them well educated and trained in U.S. universities, should continue to drive American innovation and productivity in future decades.

Figure 1-24 Life Expectancy Rates at Birth: 2009 Estimates

Country	Total Population	Males	Females
Canada	81.2	78.7	83.9
China	73.5	71.6	75.5
France	81.0	77.8	84.3
Germany	79.3	76.3	82.4
Ireland	78.2	75.6	81.1
Israel	80.7	78.6	83.0
Japan	82.1	78.8	85.6
Netherlands	79.4	76.8	82.1
Spain	80.1	76.7	83.6
Switzerland	80.9	78.0	83.8
United Kingdom	79.0	76.5	81.6
United States	78.1	75.7	80.7

Source: Central Intelligence Agency

Depth and Breadth of Markets

The depth and breadth of financial and other markets will also no doubt continue to favor the United States in future decades. The American stock market's capitalization is almost four times that of China, Japan, or the United Kingdom and more than three times that of the eurozone stock exchanges (Figure 1-10). In terms of net government debt in the hands of individual and institutional investors, and therefore available for foreign traders and investors, the United States also dominates (Figure 1-9). And note that second-place Japan, with huge government debt after years of deficit spending in attempts to revive the economy, has only 6 percent of its debt owned by foreigners (Figure 1-25). The rest is held internally—hardly an earmark of an international currency. In contrast, 46 percent of Treasuries are owned abroad.

Figure 1-25 Japanese Government Bondholders (September 2011)

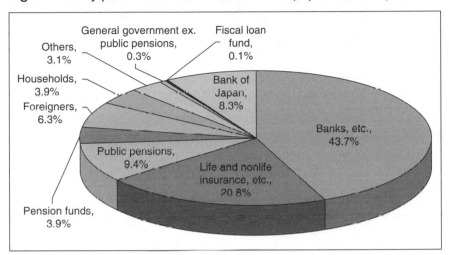

Source: Bank of Japan

Free and Open Markets

The United States' free and open financial markets also favor the dollar as the primary international trade and reserve currency in coming years. In contrast, Chinese financial markets and the yuan are tightly controlled by the government, although some gradual liberalization is occurring, largely through Hong Kong. But with limited exceptions, foreigners cannot invest in mainland equities and other securities. And in the main, Chinese citizens cannot invest offshore.

I've suggested that if they could, the yuan might fall as the heavily saving Chinese moved money out of the country in order to diversify. At present, their limited choices are all unattractive. Chinese stocks are volatile and declining, with the Shanghai Composite Index dropping 22 percent in 2011. With high inflation and low interest rates, bank deposits earn a distinctly negative real return.

Interest rates are kept low to provide cheap financing by the state banks—in effect, subsidized by consumers—for the many inefficient state-owned enterprises that need low interest costs if they are to survive, but that are essential to the government, since they employ lots of people and account for about 50 percent of GDP. Keeping people employed is Job One for Chinese leaders, who are well aware that the 1989 Tiananmen Square uprising was sparked by high unemployment problems.

The remaining major area for investment by Chinese households is real estate, and the recent boom shows that this was the investment of choice for savers and the outlet for much of the $285 billion fiscal stimulus in 2009, the equivalent of 12 percent of Chinese GDP and twice the size of the U.S. program that same year in relation to the economy. However, leaping prices bother the government, which hates speculation and promotes egalitarianism. It has moved to curb prices, even though similar restraints in 2008 led to a collapse. Second-home buyers must now put down 50 percent of the purchase price compared to 30 percent for first-time home buyers. The government is also pressing banks to contain mortgage lending, and some banks have recently raised mortgage rates. Also, new taxes are being imposed on residential property.

Far from being free and open, about 40 percent of new Chinese bank loans in the first half of 2011 were shadow finance loans, often made to smaller private firms and then moved off their books into wealth management products that offer higher interest rates than the banks are allowed to pay directly. Including these, the IMF estimates that total bank loans were 173 percent of GDP at the end of June, an "unusually high level" for a developing country, the IMF states. As part of the efforts to slow the economy, the China Banking Regulatory Commission recently banned banks from this practice and is requiring banks to bring these assets back onto their balance sheets. Shadow financing accounts for about 20 percent of total bank loans.

The Yuan

In 1993, the Chinese devalued the yuan by 50 percent; it went from 5.81 to 8.72 per dollar (Figure 1-26). That put other Asian lands at an export disadvantage and, in addition to excessive reliance on borrowing abroad in hard currencies, may have been an important cause of the 1997–1998 financial and economic collapse in Asia. In any event, the yuan was pegged until 2005, when the Chinese government, under intense pressure from the United States and Europe to curb China's huge and growing trade surplus, allowed it to rise in a controlled manner to 6.8 per dollar in mid-2008, an increase of 21 percent. But with the global recession and weakness in the Chinese economy and in exports, the government again pegged the yuan to the greenback.

Figure 1-26 Chinese Yuan per U.S. Dollar

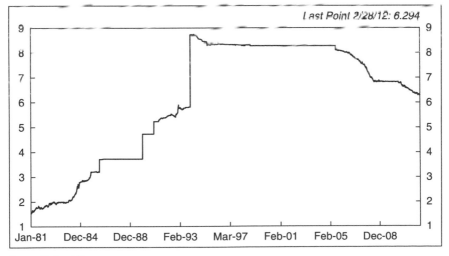

Source: Federal Reserve

In 2009–2010, China faced renewed pressure from Europe and the United States to move its currency higher, and in June 2010, it again moved up the yuan against the greenback by 7.1 percent through October 2011. But on October 11, the U.S. Senate passed a bill that would penalize China for holding down the value of its currency, and in the next two days, the Chinese government pushed the yuan lower, not higher, against the dollar. Chinese leaders obviously wanted to show that they control their currency and aren't going to be pushed around by foreigners. This is clearly the opposite behavior from that of a government that's promoting its currency as an international standard.

Persisting Attitudes

These Chinese attitudes are likely to persist for decades and prevent the yuan from becoming an international trading and reserve currency, despite statements to the contrary by government officials. The Chinese well remember their "century of humiliation" touched off by the nineteenth-century Opium Wars, after which the British, joined by the Americans and French, forced huge trading concessions on China.

This humiliation came on top of the Chinese memories that five centuries earlier, China had been ahead of the West in living standards and technology. But then the country stagnated, in part because its rulers decided that life was as good as it could get and that any further changes would be detrimental. The West, however, really took off in the 1800s with the Industrial Revolution, which allowed it to dominate China by military force.

Lack of Substitutes

Lack of substitutes is also likely to keep the greenback on the international currency throne for many years. The U.S. economy, government policies, and, therefore, the dollar are not in great shape these days, but the greenback remains the best of a bad lot: the least bad choice, the cleanest shirt in the dirty clothes bin, the slowest-dropping rock, and the best horse in the glue factory. Witness the fact that in May 2010, the Fed reinstated swap agreements to supply European banks, by way of the ECB, with dollars that they desperately need, now that U.S. money market funds and others have cut off loans to problematic eurozone institutions. Today, the buck is the only meaningful currency that's in short supply.

The only possible contenders to the dollar as the global reserve and transactions currency are the Chinese yuan, the Japanese yen, and the euro. The Indian rupee is also a possibility, but not for the many, many years it will take the Indian economy to achieve world-class status (Figure 1-19). Let's examine each of these possibilities.

The Yuan

The Chinese say that they eventually want the yuan to become a reserve currency, in keeping with the country's growing economic power. A year ago, the chairman of state-controlled China Construction Bank said that pressure for China to play a more active role in reshaping the global financial system should be matched by willingness to change the system to accommodate China. By saying that the global financial community should move toward including the yuan as a reserve currency, he implied that major developed countries should hold yuan in their currency reserves in return for China's holding dollars and other currencies. He also said that the yuan should be immediately included in the IMF's Special Drawing Rights currency basket, as the governor of China's central bank had also said earlier.

As the old saying goes, however, actions speak louder than words, and Chinese actions and attitudes indicate no interest in opening the country's currency and financial markets, as is required of an international currency. China runs a mercantilist system that would have made the eighteenth-century French green with envy. It basically imports raw materials and the equipment needed to turn them into manufactured exports. With the retrenchment of U.S. consumers who bought most of those exports directly or indirectly in earlier years, China needs to move toward a domestically driven economy, but it will take many years before consumer spending reaches Western shares of GDP.

Meanwhile, China runs its economy with little regard for international free-trade norms. Earlier, because of "environmental concerns" (and not, of course, to control world trade), it restricted the production and export of rare earths, which are predominantly mined and refined in China. China also has a stop-go economic policy that is not attractive to foreign investors and currency holders. In reaction to the 2007–2009 global recession and retrenchment of U.S. consumers, it embarked on a massive stimulus largely through bank lending, which surged $1.4 trillion, or 32 percent, over the course of 2009 after having been flat since 2006, while the money supply leaped by 29 percent.

Quick Results

A tightly controlled economy can get results quickly, and that's what happened in China. Unlike the $787 billion U.S. fiscal effort that same year, China's stimulus faced no arguing in congressional committees, no need to wait for environmental approvals before infrastructure projects could be announced, and no holdups because mortgage lenders didn't have the staffs to modify mortgages. Then, in response to the inflation and real estate booms that accompanied rapid economic revival, China has slammed on the brakes. The goal is to reduce real GDP growth to about the 8 percent needed to accommodate new job seekers, but I am looking for a hard landing, with growth dropping to 5 to 6 percent, as occurred in the Great Recession (Figure 1-27). That's a major recession in China.

Effecting a soft landing is extremely difficult, in part because China's policy tools are extremely crude. The central bank relies on adjusting reserve requirements and placing limits on on- and off-the-books bank lending to implement monetary policy. Since January 2010, it has raised reserve requirements 12 times, from 15.5 percent to 21.5 percent, before reducing them to 21.0 percent in late 2011.

Figure 1-27   Chinese GDP

(Year/Year Percent Change)

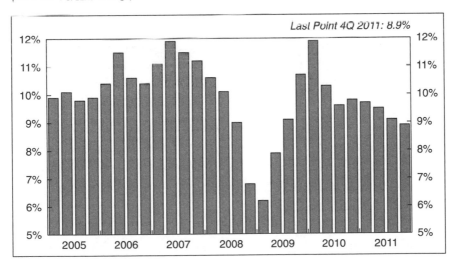

Source: Chinese National Bureau of Statistics

In contrast, the central bank hiked lending rates only five times, to 6.56 percent from 5.31 percent, in order to accommodate inefficient state enterprise borrowers that employ lots of people. Recall that the Fed hasn't changed reserve requirements in decades and considers such changes to be crude, caveman tactics. Reserve requirements limit bank lending, since they amount to credit rationing, while higher interest rates still accommodate the most promising investments.

By my reckoning, in the post–World War II era, the Fed tried 12 times to slow an overheating economy without precipitating a recession. But it succeeded only once, in the mid-1990s; the other 11 times ended in recessions. Can the nonindependent Chinese central bank and the political leaders who really call the monetary shots be more successful with their crude policy tools than the independent, sophisticated Fed?

Controls and Markets

Furthermore, implementing any economic policy in an economy that is partly top-down controlled and partly free-market driven is tough. In a completely controlled economy, as China's used to be, the leaders may make economically inefficient decisions, but their authority is not disputed—that is, by those who want to stay out of jail and continue to live. In an open economy, as in Singapore, the markets make the decisions, for better or for worse, and politicians aren't involved. But in a partly open, partly market-driven economy, as is currently the case in China, government leaders making major decisions have to guess at market responses and unintended consequences.

With a "managed floating exchange rate," for example, they have to estimate how much hot money, the flood of speculative capital from around the world, will enter China in anticipation of a stronger currency, and then figure out how to neutralize any undesired consequences. Capital control makes it hard to bring hot money into China, but speculators have used regulatory loopholes to circumvent the rules. The weak yuan, protectionism, and other policies that encourage exports and trade surpluses have pushed China's foreign currency reserves to $3.18 trillion in December 2011, up $334 billion from a year earlier. Until recently, all the foreign currency earnings of Chinese exporters had to be traded in for yuan, but then the central bank was forced to issue securities to sop up those funds that otherwise would have mushroomed the money supply. This magnified the central bank's challenge in curtailing credit growth in order to fight inflation and real estate speculation.

A hard landing in China, defined as a sharp and swift drop in economic growth, will no doubt precipitate another massive stimulus program, and the government is already taking preliminary steps in that direction. The leaders of the Mao Dynasty, as we've dubbed it, want to keep their jobs by holding down unemployment. Still, they are unlikely to react to a softening economy fast enough to prevent a hard landing and the resulting collapse in the underpinnings of the global commodities bubble.

No Decoupling

It's also hard to envision a global currency for a country that depends on exports for economic growth. That makes China and other export-driven developing countries dependent on developed lands, especially the United States. They are not yet industrialized enough to have the vast middle classes that are needed to create economies that are led by domestic spending, as discussed earlier.

The Yen

International investors have certainly favored the yen over the last two decades—despite the collapse in Japanese stocks and land prices (Figures 1-28 and 1-29) after the 1980s bubble economy burst. And, this has happened despite the sluggish economic growth and deflation since then, even in the face of huge government deficit spending that has exploded debt (Figure 1-30) and aggressive monetary policy. And, it has happened despite Japan's very low fertility rate (Figure 1-23) and falling population, and despite the perennially low Japanese interest rates.

Apparently, investors like the stability of virtually no-growth Japan in a sea of global turmoil. In any event, I argued in my recent book *The Age of Deleveraging: Investment Strategies for a Decade of Slow Growth and Deflation* (Hoboken, NJ: John Wiley & Sons, 2010), that Japan's Achilles' heel is its reliance on domestic funds to finance its ongoing huge government

Figure 1-28   Nikkei 225 Index

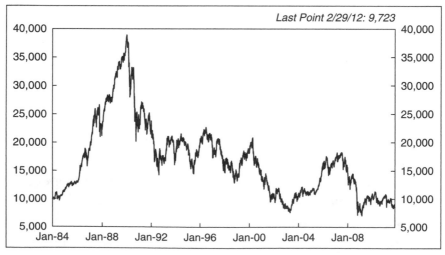

Source: Yahoo! Finance

Figure 1-29   Japanese Urban Land Prices

(Six-City Average; 1Q 2000 = 100)

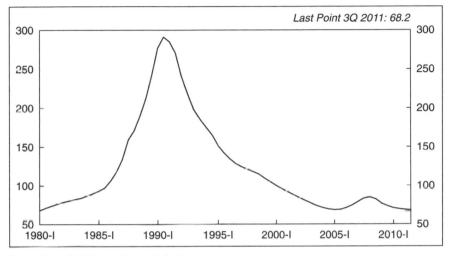

Source: Japan Real Estate Research Institute

Figure 1-30   Debt as a Percent of GDP, 2010

(OECD Gross, OECD Net, IMF Gross, IMF Net)

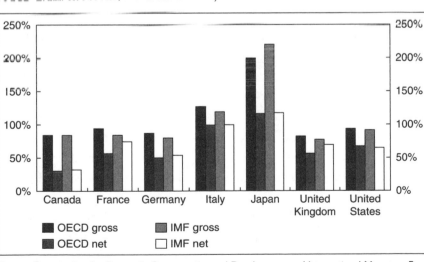

Sources: Organisation for Economic Co-operation and Development and International Monetary Fund

Figure 1-31   Japanese Saving Rate

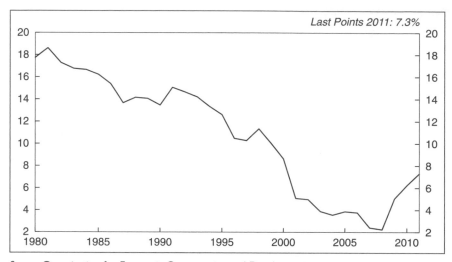

Source: Organisation for Economic Co-operation and Development

deficits. In the 1980s, the funds needed for this came from high household saving (Figure 1-31), but that source has faded as the rapidly aging population draws on its savings in retirement, as the stagnant economy reduces the ability to save, as the costs of old-age pensions and public long-term-care insurance increase, and as Japanese consumers progressively favor the good life now, with less concern for the future.

I also noted in that book that in recent years, business saving has replaced household saving in funding government deficits, as cash flow exceeds business investment. But that cash flow depends on exports in export-led Japan (Figure 1-32). So as U.S. consumers continue to retrench and negatively affect Japanese exports, corporate cash flow will fall and the current account balance will go negative (Figure 1-33). That will shift Japan from being a capital exporter to being a capital importer, pushing up bond yields (Figure 1-34) and government interest costs substantially. Not a happy prospect.

Figure 1-32 Japanese Real GDP and Exports

(Year/Year Percent Change)

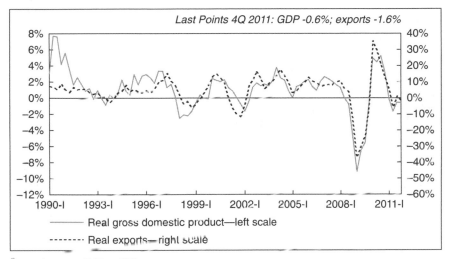

Source: Japanese Cabinet Office

Figure 1-33 Japanese Current Account and Trade Balance

(100 million yen; seasonally adjusted)

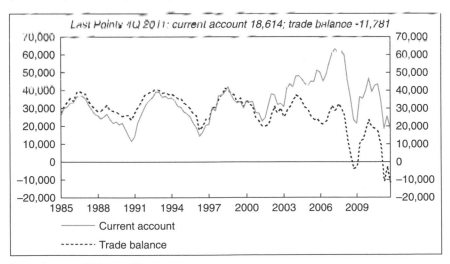

Source: Japanese Ministry of Finance

Figure 1-34 10-Year Japanese Government Bond Yields

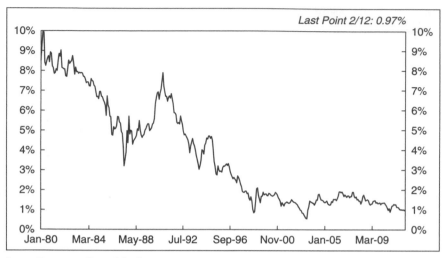

Source: European Central Bank

So the yen is an unlikely candidate to be a primary global currency, in part because of Japan's dependence on exports for economic growth. Furthermore, the Japanese, although not controlling their currency the way the Chinese do, don't favor a global reserve currency role for the yen. Exports are essential for growth, but even then, they are a relatively small part of the economy, on a par with the United States with its huge domestic economy at 12 to 15 percent of GDP. Otherwise, the Japanese remain inward-looking and suspicious of foreigners.

The Euro

Europe in general and the eurozone in particular have considerable problems that preclude the euro's becoming a major global currency any time soon, as discussed earlier. That is also probably true in the longer run as well, even though the eurozone economy is 83.5 percent as big as the U.S. economy and the population is larger. Recall that the eurozone contains very different economies, and the reason they're together under one currency is the culmination of the German and French resolve after World War II to integrate Europe's economy to reduce the risk of warfare, not because of similar cultures and economies.

The United States was fortunate to have been largely settled after the advent of the railroad. This plus Lincoln's decision to preserve the Union at all costs has given us a huge country with a basically uniform culture, one fiscal policy, and an economy so large that most businesses can achieve their full economies of scale within U.S. borders, even with today's gigantic productive potentials.

Europe, in contrast, was settled when people moved on foot or on horseback. That's heaven for American tourists. We can travel 100 miles in Europe and enjoy an entirely different culture. But it's hell for modern European businesses and for coordinated fiscal policy. And while the first decade under the common euro appears to have exacerbated the inconsistencies, global growth hid myriad eurozone problems. Indeed, in retrospect, the structure of the eurozone encouraged the divergences and imbalances that came to light when the eurozone crisis commenced in 2010.

With the huge differences in work ethics and labor structures, unit labor costs in Germany have risen 6 percent since the euro's advent, but labor costs have jumped 25 percent in France, 33 percent in Italy, 34 percent in Ireland, 36 percent in Spain, and 41 percent in Greece. Thus, Germany has been an export powerhouse while the Club Med set imported. These gulfs became especially stark as China wiped out low-tech manufacturing in Spain and Portugal, while Germany sold China the high-precision equipment used to produce those low-tech exports.

No Devaluations

If they had had their own currencies, the weak economies would have devalued—numerous times, no doubt—in the last 13 years to redress these imbalances. But with the common currency, they couldn't. Cutting wages is just too painful politically, although Ireland has done so, but only in reaction to its financial and economic near collapse. Ireland is grouped with the southern economies, but maybe there's something to be said for its northern location!

In any event, the easier way out was to borrow, and the low euro interest rates inspired by the eurozone kingpin, Germany, made borrowing very attractive for the Club Med lands. In the 2000s, low euro interest rates, combined with high inflation in Spain, yielded negative real rates, which propelled excessive borrowing and a Spanish housing boom. Furthermore, lax lending rules allowed banks in Ireland, Spain, Germany, and France to load up on risky domestic mortgages as well as Greek and Portuguese government debt. That certainly encouraged Club Med profligacy. Greece, Portugal, and Spain also benefited from getting more from the EU budget than they contributed to it.

For a common currency to work without fiscal integration, the business cycles of the countries involved need to be roughly in sync, workers need to be able to move freely and easily across borders to even out labor imbalances, and wages and prices need to be flexible. If these conditions aren't fully met, mechanisms must be available to redress the imbalances by the transfer of resources. These conditions are far from being met in the eurozone.

Forget the Rules

The fiscal rules of the EU Stability and Growth Pact that were supposed to keep economies and finances in line—government deficits limited to 3 percent of GDP and debt-to-GDP ratios of no more than 40 percent—have been ignored. Wage and price flexibility within the eurozone is limited, and migration is largely a myth, since language barriers and vast cultural differences impede labor mobility. Sicilians seldom move out of their own villages and don't speak German or like bratwurst. Therefore, they are highly unlikely to transfer to work in Germany, even though employees are allowed to move freely throughout the 27-country EU. Furthermore, the Germans and other Europeans are distinctly negative on immigration. Germany's immigration rules are very strict, despite its declining population and future need for skilled workers. Since 2008, more non-Europeans have been leaving Germany than have been entering it.

In October 2010, Chancellor Merkel said that multiculturalism in Germany had been a "total failure," adding, "for a while, we kidded ourselves into believing that they wouldn't stay and would leave. Naturally, the notion that we would live next to another and be happy about one another failed."

Emphasis on regulation rather than free markets in Europe also stifles the labor-market reforms needed to improve competitiveness. The costs of labor remain so high that many people go unhired even in boom times, and government costs for the unemployed continue to drag on those economies. Labor productivity growth rates in Europe have fallen since 1995, going from 1.5 percent annual rate from 1995–2000 to 1.1 percent per year in 2000–2005 to 0.6 percent annually in 2005–2010. The Germans became so concerned about local businesses moving production abroad that the government eased restrictive labor rules a decade ago, with notable success.

In the United States, government policy has never put a lot of weight on guaranteeing incomes, but it goes to great lengths to ensure that when consumers spend their money, it will be in free and competitive markets, unencumbered by cartels. Europe has basically taken the reverse approach to the situation. Incomes are supported through curbs on layoffs, maximum workweeks, and large and long-lived unemployment benefits, but cartels in the markets in which consumers buy are relatively unchecked. Germany vigorously restricts discounts and rebates. Clearance sales are limited to several per year. From an economist's viewpoint, the U.S. system is better and more efficient because it relies on free markets, allows unencumbered consumer choice, and lets prices effectively relay economic preferences to producers.

Two Choices

The current eurozone structure has proved to be unfeasible, so two long-run choices remain: allow and encourage weak members to leave the common currency, or move toward much more complete fiscal and even political integration to curb nonstop bailouts of the weaker economies. Departures would create a big mess, as noted earlier.

Further and substantial fiscal and monetary integration is probably preferable to the demise of the eurozone, but it is also packed with problems. Former ECB president Trichet made a plea for further integration his swan song. Tacitly acknowledging that Europe's institutional structures have failed, he called for a "new type of confederation of sovereign states." He wanted a new ministry of finance with powers to override governments that receive aid but don't live up to their promised reforms. He also wanted a fully integrated European banking system. In March 2011, Trichet told finance ministers that attempts to tighten sanctions are "insufficient" because they don't apply to wayward countries automatically and are subject to intervention by politicians. A very Germanic Frenchman!

The IMF also desires further integration in Europe to avoid financial crises with "major global consequences." It wants to reduce national sovereignty in the eurozone by having central authorities conduct more stringent surveillance of members' budgets, have more input into national policies, and issue debt.

The problem with these proposals is that to many of the smaller and weaker countries, they look like a European takeover by the Teutonic north, especially by Germany. The Greeks, remembering the German occupation in World War II, don't want to be made into Germans by Germany. And it's probably true that Germany, perhaps in conjunction with France, would call the shots.

In 2011, smaller eurozone countries chafed at the plan by Germany and France to impose common economic measures to improve the competitiveness of the weak sisters. The German proposals, backed by France, would have made expansion of the bailout fund conditional on raising retirement ages across the eurozone, eliminating indexing of wages to inflation, harmonizing corporate and other taxes, and instituting limits on deficit financing to fund spending.

Credibility

Credibility is on my list of six criteria for a primary global trading and reserve currency. There can't be major concerns about the country's devaluing or otherwise debasing its currency. This, of course, is the vulnerable spot for the dollar, which has been falling against other major currencies on a trade-weighted basis since 1985 (Figure 1-14). In that year, major country officials hammered out the Plaza Accord (since they met at the Plaza Hotel in New York City), which called for coordinated efforts to push down what was regarded as an overly robust buck. My recollection is that the dollar was already starting to weaken, and that those officials simply climbed aboard the moving freight train and took credit for getting it rolling.

In any event, further attempts to devalue the greenback, either unilaterally by the United States or in concert with other nations, seem highly unlikely, unless it strengthens fantastically. Furthermore, attempts to debase the buck by deliberately promoting inflation to reduce its purchasing power against other currencies is something I've never heard even mentioned, much less seriously discussed, in Washington. And with my forecast of deflation, they probably couldn't pull off the desired effect of inflation and growth if they tried.

In *The Age of Deleveraging*, I identified seven forms of inflation/deflation, and in the October 2011 edition of my monthly newsletter, "Insight," I noted that five forms of deflation are underway.

1. *Financial asset deflation* started with the nosedive in subprime mortgages in early 2007. Now it's rampant in the collapsed prices of Greek sovereign debt and European bank stocks, and in the balance sheets of European and U.S. banks as they dump assets. U.S. private and public pension funds have been deflated by falling Treasury yields. Stocks are deflating universally in response to global economic weakness, eurozone woes, and the prospective hard landing in China.
2. *Tangible asset deflation* is proceeding, and U.S. house prices are likely to fall another 20 percent (Figure 1-35). Commercial real estate prices are down 43 percent. Housing bubbles are bursting or at risk in Spain and China.

Figure 1-35   Case-Shiller 10-City House Price Index

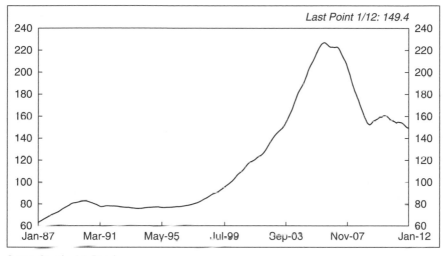

Source: Standard & Poor's

3. *Commodity deflation* is in full flower as industrial
    commodities, led by copper, grains, and even gold,
    nosedive (Figure 1-36). A hard landing in China and
    collapsed commodity demand will crumble the
    foundation of the commodity bubble.
4. *U.S. wages and incomes are deflating,* with real median
    household income declining (Figure 1-37) as high
    unemployment and weak labor demand persist.
    Household net worth is down 23 percent from its fourth-
    quarter 2006 peak and, relative to disposable personal
    income, is lower than in the 1950s. Income polarization
    persists, and the middle class is being deflated to low-
    income status.
5. *Foreign currencies are deflating* against the dollar, the only
    global reserve currency and the ultimate safe haven.
    Also, the euro is mired in sovereign debt crises,

Figure 1-36 Reuters/Jefferies Commodity Research Bureau Index

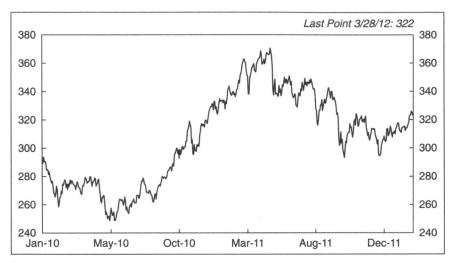

Source: Jefferies & Co.

Figure 1-37 Real Median Household Income

(2010 $)

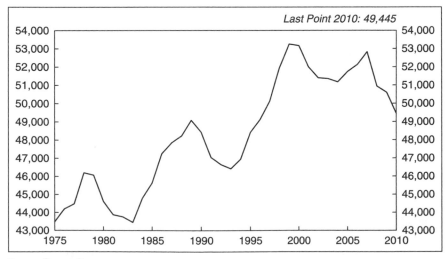

Source: Census Bureau

commodity-based currencies are dropping, and even the Chinese yuan is problematic.

6. *Inflation by fiat* still reigns as government laws and regulations hype costs and wages. This includes increasing minimum wages, requiring higher gas mileage for vehicles, protectionist measures, agricultural price supports, the Dodd-Frank regulations, and all the other ways in which the government, with the stroke of a pen, raises prices by interrupting free markets. The 2012 election, however, may spawn genuine tax simplification and other forms of deflation by fiat.

7. *Goods and services deflation*, the seventh variety and the one that most people think of in terms of consumer or producer prices when then they refer to deflation, has not yet arrived. But with deflation in financial and tangible assets, commodities, real wages, and currencies underway, it can't be far behind. As global deleveraging persists, goods and services prices will be marked down to reestablish equilibrium. With house prices, stocks, commodity prices, and household purchasing power all falling, how can wholesale and consumer prices resist the onslaught when consumers are trying to save and cut debt, not spend freely? The Fed, in its September 21, 2011 policy statement, in effect expressed renewed concern over goods and services deflation.

Current Account Deficit

Until the recent rally, the dollar had declined for 25 years, and many people consider this a deliberate debasement of the currency. They also see the chronic foreign trade and current account deficits (Figure 1-1) as a major reason. Note, however, that the rest of the world depends on the United States to buy its excess goods and services, and the American trade deficit of $720 billion over the last 12 months is the counterpart to surpluses elsewhere. The effects of the recently sluggish U.S. economy as well as recession-bound Europe on emerging economies and their securities markets show the export dependence of Asian and other lands on developed country importers, especially America.

Furthermore, as Belgian-American economist Robert Triffin pointed out in the 1960s, the country whose currency is the global reserve currency must be willing to run current account deficits to supply the reserve currency demanded by other countries. This is known as the Triffin dilemma because of the conflicting goals of a current account surplus to promote a strong currency and the need to run a deficit to meet the needs of foreign holders of that reserve currency. In the case of the dollar, many of those foreign reserves are held in the form of Treasuries.

The Triffin dilemma also explains, at least in part, why the U.S. trade and current account deficits have not been self-correcting, despite the declining dollar. A falling greenback is supposed to boost U.S. exports and economic activity while weakening imports and therefore economic activity in foreign countries. That, the theory goes, should induce interest-rate cuts abroad to rejuvenate those economies while interest rates rise in America, and the shift in interest-rate spreads in America's favor should make U.S. investments more attractive. Also, faster growth here than overseas is expected to attract foreign money. The net effect is to strengthen the dollar as money moves from abroad to the United States and reestablish equilibrium.

Recycled Dollars

By definition, the U.S. current account deficit must be recycled back into dollar investments, which can range from currency to Treasuries to U.S. corporate stocks and bonds to Iowa farmland. The only alternative is to convert it to paper dollar bills, cut them up with scissors, and flush them down the toilet. If the Taiwanese don't want to invest their dollar current account surplus in greenback-denominated assets, they could trade their dollars for Swiss francs, but then the seller of those Swiss francs would have the responsibility for recycling the dollars. Of course, in the recycling process, foreign dollar holders can determine the buck's relative value, but that doesn't change the necessity of keeping their dollar current account surpluses in dollar assets.

Many people worry that big foreign holders of dollars, especially the Chinese, will dump their Treasuries and other dollar assets for political reasons. Accidents can and do happen, but such attempts could be suicidal. If foreigners refused to recycle their ongoing trade surpluses with the United States into American investments and tried to dump their existing holdings of Treasuries and other American assets as well, the dollar would collapse, and so would global financial markets and the global economy. The export-led developing countries, first and foremost China, would be the biggest losers, while the United States and other developed lands would fare better.

But no one wants that, and—short of panic, which is always a risk—no one will precipitate it. Foreigners now hold almost half of U.S. Treasury bonds, about 10 percent of American stocks, and better than a third of corporate bonds. Also, where would they go if they vacated the dollar? The Swiss franc and gold are much too small markets to accommodate the holders of foreign dollars.

It's ironic that the United States, with its chronic trade and current account deficits and the resulting big holdings of American assets by foreigners, has more power in the international trade game than the foreign holders of these assets. But in a world of surplus goods and services, the buyer, not the seller, has the upper hand. Just ask any successful salesperson.

The U.S. current account and trade deficits are likely to fall in future years. Consumer retrenchment will retard imports, and therefore these deficits will fall, assuming that foreigners continue to buy U.S. exports. For every 1 percent decline in consumer spending, U.S. imports fall 2.8 percent on average. Furthermore, while globalization has eliminated labor-intensive U.S. manufacturing, the manufacturing that remains is highly productive. The Boston Consulting Group believes that seven industries may see production for U.S. consumers move from China back to the United States: furniture, transportation equipment, computers and electronics, electrical equipment and appliances, plastics and rubber products, machinery, and fabricated metal products. Rising labor costs in China will work to the advantage of American competitors, as will transportation costs, closer proximity to U.S. markets, and other such factors.

Furthermore, net physical barrels of crude oil and petroleum products imports have fallen 41 percent since August 2006 as a result of the weak U.S. economy, more conservation, and rising domestic production. Petroleum imports dropped from 60 percent of total supply in 2005 to 49 percent in 2010. As these trends persist, the petroleum trade deficit, which was $27.6 billion in November 2011 and 58 percent of the $47.7 billion total, will decline, assuming that oil prices don't spike, thereby reducing U.S. trade red ink.

On Balance

On balance, the credibility factor is the only one of my six criteria for a primary international trading and reserve currency on which the dollar is at all questionable in the years ahead. Because of the United States' superior prospective productivity growth, huge economic size, and deep and broad as well as open and free markets, the American currency should persist as the unchallenged winner. And the credibility issue will probably continue to be noncrucial because there will probably be no global alternative to the buck for many years to come.

CHAPTER 2

THE WORLD'S HEGEMONIC RESERVE CURRENCY: THE U.S. DOLLAR VERSUS THE CHINESE YUAN

Stephen L. Jen

"*The growing question is whether the exceptional role of the dollar can be maintained.*"

Paul Volcker, former Federal Reserve Chairman,
November 31, 2010

The global financial crisis of 2008 has made it tempting to discount the long-term prospect of everything American. In addition to the derating of the United States' economic, political, and military dominance, many people argue that the dollar will soon lose its hegemony, or authoritative dominance, as a reserve and international currency. At the same time, in part because of the powerful rise of China in the past decade, some people believe that the yuan could soon become a major reserve currency, perhaps challenging the dollar in that role within the decade.

While the rise of China's economy and the growing international role of the yuan are compelling generational trends, it may be a mistake to underestimate the durability of the dollar as the dominant reserve currency and overestimate the speed with which the yuan could become a dominant reserve currency.

Here are five thoughts.

1. It Is a Mistake to Think that the Reserve Currency Dominance Has Much to Do with the Relative Size of the Economy

In purchasing power parity (PPP) terms, China's economy is already 70 percent that of the United States, and it is projected to surpass the United States' by 2016. Some have argued that, simply because of the sheer size of the Chinese economy, the yuan will, almost as a matter of course, become the dominant reserve currency. However, looking at the various reserve currencies in the world, there does not appear to be a tight relationship between the size of the economy and its reserve currency status. For example, in terms of nominal GDP, the United States is slightly smaller than the European Economic and Monetary Union (EMU), yet its share of global reserves is more than twice as large. Switzerland's economy is 8 percent the size of Japan's, yet the Swiss franc, as a reserve currency, has almost as big an international market share as the yen. At present, the yuan accounts for zero percent of the world's reserves; it is much harder to manufacture a reserve currency than it is to manufacture goods.

Without a stringent application of the rule of law, accounting transparency, and sufficient liquidity in the underlying markets (bond and equity markets), it will be difficult for emerging-market economies in general to *make*—by mandate or by size—their currencies "reserve" currencies. Fixating on the size of the economy in this discussion is like judging the value of a car based on only its top speed, ignoring other criteria such as handling, reliability, safety, and comfort.

It is difficult to be the hegemonic reserve currency of the world. Importantly, the issuing country must have (1) liquid capital markets, (2) a relatively stable economic regime, (3) a sustainable political regime, and (4) a mighty military force. Neither the eurozone, China, Japan, nor Russia possesses *all four* of these criteria. China may have an enviable production-export industrial complex, but it does not yet have a yield curve* that is meaningful or viable. In fact, in many of the emerging-market economies, the development of the capital markets has in general lagged badly behind the developments of the real sector; this is like someone having the upper body of a body builder but the legs of a 12-year-old boy. Why else would China—supposedly the future issuer of the dominant reserve currency in the world—need to have US$3.5 trillion in reserves for self-insurance purposes?† These countries rely on

---

* The yield curve is the relationship between the level of the interest rate and the time to maturity. Specifically, it is the array of short-term and long-term interest rates.

† Emerging-market central banks accumulate foreign reserves—mostly in U.S. dollars—to guard against sudden capital flight triggered by a loss of confidence on the part of foreign investors. This is called *self-insurance* because many emerging-market central banks have tried to minimize the use of resources from the International Monetary Fund (IMF) or other international institutions by stockpiling foreign reserves themselves.

the U.S. dollar as the currency to use in the event of an emergency precisely because it is superior to and more trustworthy than the yuan.

Perhaps *the* critical issue for the yuan and other emerging-market currencies that might aim to challenge the dollar is not the size of their economies or their trade, but the size and liquidity of their financial markets. The bond markets of the top five reserve currencies (the U.S. dollar [USD], the euro [EUR], the Japanese yen [JPY], the British pound [GBP], and the Swiss franc [CHF]) account for some 90 percent of the world's sovereign bond liquidity, and more than two-thirds of the equity-market liquidity. While these top five reserve currency issuers account for only 36 percent of the world's trade, they account for 81 percent of the currency transactions and 96 percent of the world's foreign reserves. The gap in terms of the level of development and openness of the financial markets is one of the key defining differences between developed and emerging markets. Unless China, India, Brazil, and others can offer the world full access to their financial markets, and actively nurture these markets to make them large and liquid, it will be very difficult for their currencies to become dominant international currencies in the near future.

2. It Is a Mistake to Underestimate the Incumbency Advantage

The half-century lag between the milestone of the United States surpassing the United Kingdom (in terms of size of economy and volume of trade) and the dollar finally replacing the pound sterling as the leading reserve currency after World War II is a reminder of the immensely powerful forces of economies of scale. Children around the world—even those in China—are eagerly learning English, not because English is necessarily superior to French or Mandarin Chinese, but because everyone else in the world speaks English. The dollar is "English" in the currency world. Similarly, it makes sense to price commodities in the most widely used currency in the world—the dollar: it would be odd to mandate that oil and gold be priced in Special Drawing Rights (SDRs) of the International Monetary Fund (IMF) just so that we could be politically correct or "democratic." The U.S. dollar enjoys a tremendous advantage in its use as an international currency because there are so many dollars circulating. Even if the U.S. dollar does lose its hegemonic reserve currency status (a consensus view), I believe that this will be an extremely gradual process (an out-of-consensus view).

The dollar's international reserve currency status should be judged on its role as (1) a medium of exchange, (2) a unit of account, and (3) a store of value. On points 1 and 2, I think it will be extremely difficult for the U.S. dollar to cede its lead to any rival currency. It is only on point 3 that the dollar has issues, which are accentuated in an increasingly multipolar world. When the global economy fell into a violent recession in 2008—one caused by the United States itself—the dollar, rather perversely, was bought as the safe haven currency. I doubt that the U.S. dollar's international reserve currency status (in the private sector, not the official sector) has deteriorated that much since then. In short, the dollar's role as (1) a medium of exchange and (2) a unit of account has been well maintained over the last 35 years.

It may be useful to examine the role of the U.S. dollar as the invoice and settlement currency not just for international trade, but also for cross-border capital flows.

There has been much angst regarding the dollar-denominated international monetary system. On August 25, 2010, French president Sarkozy announced his agenda for France's then-forthcoming presidency of the G-20 Group, which would include a discussion on a comprehensive overhaul of this dollar-dominated system. On August 28, 2010, the IMF's first deputy managing director, John Lipsky, delivered a speech on a similar topic and touched on the international role of the dollar. Furthermore, there have been ample reports of countries promoting the settlement of regional trade in local currencies, not in dollars. For example, in the past two years, China has signed numerous agreements with its contiguous trading partners to settle border trade in local currencies, bypassing the dollar. On July 2, 2009, China and Brazil announced their agreement to settle some of their trade in their own currencies, instead of the dollar.* Moreover, China has also announced important steps toward greater internationalization of the yuan by liberalizing the capital account.†

The powerful and irreversible trend toward general diversification away from the dollar is clear, except that this consensus view is not supported by data.

---

* I note that the actual currency settlement arrangement is much more complicated than what one might assume. It does not entail Brazilian exporters receiving BRL (Brazilian reals) from Chinese importers. Rather, the process entails a complex series of transactions and guarantees from the official sectors of the two countries.

† China liberalized its foreign exchange settlement arrangements with Malaysia, and McDonald's issued bonds in yuans to finance its operations in China. Previously, nonfinancial foreign-owned entities had to borrow in dollars to fund these operations. China is also relaxing its restrictions on foreign central banks and investors participating in the interbank bond market. These steps should help provide an investment opportunity for foreign entities that have accumulated yuan through trade.

There is perhaps not a sufficient appreciation for the relative size of international trade and international capital flows. It is well known that global trade has surged sharply in the last decade, reflecting in part China's entry into the World Trade Organization (WTO) in 2001 and its subsequent ascendancy. Global exports grew strongly from US$6.1 trillion a year in 2001 to US$15 trillion a year at the end of 2010—a cumulative 100 percent increase over the decade.* If more and more of global trade is being denominated and settled in currencies other than the dollar, surely the dollar's hegemonic status is being eroded, or so the argument goes.

The problem with this argument is that it misses the key point that international *trade* accounts for only a tiny fraction of total currency transactions, and that international *capital* flows dominate the currency markets.

Figure 2-1   Trends in Foreign Exchange and Trade Transactions

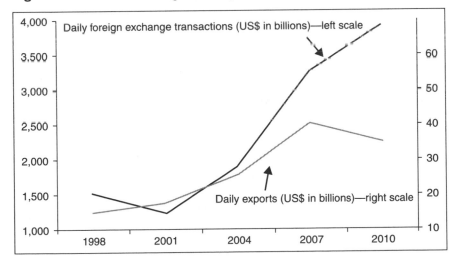

---

* In this note, we discuss global exports rather than global trade, as the former is simply half of the latter.

In late 2010, the Bank for International Settlements (BIS) issued its latest "Triennial Central Bank Survey" on global foreign exchange transactions, which have registered a cumulative 220 percent growth since 2001, reaching US$4.0 trillion a day as of the end of April 2010. In comparison, global exports are around US$40 billion a day. This makes international trade a mere 2 percent of total currency transactions, suggesting that 98 percent of all currency transactions are related to capital flows, hedging, and other activities that are not directly linked to trade settlement. Figure 2-1 shows not only that international capital flows are 50 times as large as international trade flows, but that they have grown more than twice as fast as the rapid trade growth in the past decade (220 percent growth for capital flows, compared to 100 percent growth in international trade). (The ratio of capital flows to trade flows was 35:1 back in 2001.)

Thus, even if the dollar may lose its international status as a *trade* settlement currency within Asia, it will take much more for it to lose the *capital flow* settlement currency status in Asia, in my opinion, as the dollar is still the dominant currency for capital flows.*

3. It Is a Mistake to Write Off the U.S. Dollar, Again

The world has underestimated the dollar's hegemonic international currency status before; it just doesn't remember that it has done so.

---

* According to the BIS "Triennial Central Bank Survey," for the past 15 years, the market share of the U.S. dollar in cross-border transactions has remained unchanged at around 85 percent, despite globalization and multipolarism of the global economy, and the yuan currently accounts for about 0.3 percent of the total currency turnover, despite the size of the Chinese economy.

The IMF's COFER* data have attracted a great deal of attention in recent years, in light of the multiyear dollar correction that began in 2001 and the sharp rise in the world's official reserve holdings. With more than US$10 trillion in assets under management, what these central bank reserve managers do matters a lot for the dollar, or so the argument goes. These COFER data show a definitive and, many find, disturbing trend decline in the past decade in the dollar's "market share" in the world's reserve holdings. Coupled with the rise of the euro and emerging markets, talk of an early demise of the dollar as the dominant international reserve currency is ripe.

I think one reason that some investors are so excited about the imminent demise of the dollar is that they are looking at the COFER data outside of the context of historical perspective. Data on currency compositions of reserves are readily available for the period 2000 onward, and indeed many focus on this period and are worried by the declining trend in the dollar's share of the world's reserves. However, with a little more effort, one can construct a longer time series for these data, going back to 1973.

Figure 2-2 is based on data from the IMF. (You can find some of these figures for the period 1973–2000 in the various back issues of the IMF's Annual Reports.) This longer time series, going back to the breakup of the Bretton Woods system in 1973, provides a proper historical context for thinking about the dollar's international status.

---

* Currency Composition of Official Foreign Exchange Reserves, published by the IMF on a quarterly basis. The IMF collates data from its member central banks on their foreign official reserve holdings, and these holdings are broken down into different currencies. Investors use these data to analyze how much of a particular reserve currency central banks are holding and how these market shares evolve over time.

Figure 2-2 Currencies' Share of Official Reserves, 1973–2009

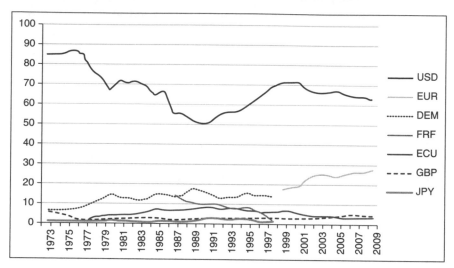

During the past 35 years, the dollar's "market share" in the world's official reserves has fluctuated between a low of 50.6 percent in 1990 and a high of 86.7 percent in 1976. Yes, it is true that its share has declined from 71.5 percent in 2001 to 62.8 percent as of Q2 2009; however, the magnitude of this recent decline is unimpressive, compared to the decline in the 1980s. Also, the current level of 62.8 percent is roughly in the middle of this 35-year range.

I have also plotted official reserves held in the euro, the German mark (DEM), the French franc (FRF), the European Currency Unit (ECU, which preceded the euro), the Japanese yen (JPY), and the British pound (GBP). These lines are clustered at the bottom of the chart. The fact that some of you will have to squint to distinguish them from one another makes the point that none of these currencies ever came close to rivaling the dollar's international dominance.

Some investors may recall that in the 1980s and the early 1990s, there were plenty of discussions about the dollar's losing its hegemonic status to the Japanese yen or the German mark, for several reasons. First, both Germany and Japan had emerged as manufacturing powerhouses that seemed to be on the path to challenging the United States' economic standing in the global economy. Second, the dollar did indeed depreciate for much of this period, unnerving long-term investors.* Third, the United States began to run large external imbalances in the early 1980s, coinciding with the rise of Germany and Japan. Indeed, as can be seen in Figure 2-2, the shares of DEM and JPY in the world's reserves did rise steadily during that period, at the expense of the U.S. dollar's share.

However, in the end, the dollar managed to maintain its dominance.

Before the European debt crisis, several scholars and commentators had used the exact same arguments to assert that the euro would one day supplant the dollar as the dominant reserve currency in the world: that the euro would first become the settlement currency in Europe, and maybe Eastern Europe. The size of Europe's population, its economic size, and the imminent demise of the U.S. empire were all used as arguments. Contrary to these confident predictions, which attracted some media attention several years ago, the euro now accounts for less than half the dollar's market share as a reserve currency—and much of the rise of the euro has

---

* The United States' current account deficit, which reflects primarily its trade deficit, has been a negative factor for the dollar. Large external imbalances need to be financed. If the net capital inflows into a country struggle to finance this external imbalance, the currency needs to depreciate to reequilibrate the external account.

been due, ironically, to China's buying, while the EMU is at risk of collapsing.* In short, many people had written off the U.S. dollar prematurely and erroneously declared that the euro would ultimately supplant the dollar's international role, partly, just as others before them had erroneously and prematurely written off the dollar in the 1980s.

4. The Excessively High Foreign Official Reserve Holdings by Many Central Banks Are a Problem

One reason that the world's central banks are diversifying their foreign reserves away from the dollar is because they have too much of them. In other words, the U.S. dollar may still be the preferred intervention currency, and the fact that central banks are diversifying away from it may reflect more their inappropriately high reserve holdings, rather than flaws in the dollar itself or its undesirability. Fixating on the dollar losing its hegemony misses the point that the *cause* of the diversification lies somewhere else.

Our calculations show that, out of the US$10 trillion in official reserves held by emerging-market economies, close to US$6.5 trillion may be considered "excessive," that is, in excess of the traditional reasons for a country to hold foreign reserves. A portion of the excess reserves was accumulated for self-insurance purposes following the Asian currency crisis of 1997, and a part has been the result of Asia's currency policy of

---

* This is ironic because EUR/USD has been supported precisely because China has accumulated too much reserves, and part of the excess reserves needed to be diversified away from the dollar.

quasi-pegs vis-à-vis the dollar. As the dollar depreciated in the past decade, Asian central banks have had to buy massive amounts of dollars to maintain this "de facto dollar peg."*

Many of these foreign reserves are not good financial investments. After the Great Recession, with developed markets being mired in disinflation and emerging markets in inflation, for the first time in recent history, Asian central banks are running a negative carry on their reserve holdings.† We calculate that it is costing China about US$110 billion a year in negative carry to hold its reserves. In general, we see merit to the notion that the countries with savings surpluses have distorted the incentives in the rest of the world through their abnormal accumulation of foreign assets. Just because a country can make money does not mean that it knows how to invest the wealth.

The definition of "foreign official reserves" needs to be clarified before a valid conversation on diversification and reserve currencies can be conducted. If more than half of the world's US$10 trillion in official reserves are excessive, conceptually, one could divide up the official reserves into two tranches: a *liquidity* tranche and an *investment* tranche, with the latter

---

* To peg one currency to another, the "pegger" needs to constantly adjust the relative supply of the local currency vis-à-vis the anchor currency. If demand for, say, the Korean won is large, and the Bank of Korea wants to prevent the won from appreciating, then it will need to increase the supply of the won and decrease the supply of the dollar. Central banks conduct market interventions by buying U.S. dollars from the market and paying for these purchases with their home currency. This is how a currency peg can be maintained. But if there is sustained strong demand for the won, then the Bank of Korea will need to be constantly in the market buying dollars. This is one way in which a central bank can end up with excess foreign reserves.
† In other words, the interest rate that China's central bank pays on the domestic bonds it issues is higher than the interest rate it earns on its U.S. Treasury holdings.

being invested the way a sovereign wealth fund (SWF) might invest: in equities, other emerging-market currencies, and so on. If the term *reserves* is properly and strictly defined as the part of the foreign reserves that is needed to meet liquidity requirements, the U.S. dollar still absolutely and definitively dominates, since potential speculative runs on the Korean won, Chinese yuan, Brazilian real, and Indian rupee will take place through the U.S. dollar, not through any other currency.

But if the Asian central banks have accumulated far more reserves than they need for liquidity purposes, and if they diversify the excess reserves into nondollar currencies and assets other than sovereign bonds, it would be misleading to conclude that this is due to the dollar and U.S. Treasuries losing their shine as reserve assets, since these assets are technically no longer reserves, defined in the strict sense. I think some people may have confused the cause and the effect in this discussion on the dollar and reserves. For what it is worth, I am of the opinion that the overaccumulation of reserves by Asia is a major policy mistake whose negative consequences will become clear over time.

5. Challenges That the Chinese Yuan Faces

In the past decade, China has risen with quiet confidence: never having boasted about what it was going to achieve, China quietly took steps to improve its economy and let the results do the talking. The scale of the eradication of abject poverty in China in the past decade is nothing less than spectacular. Domestically, the consequences of this include greater social order, ethnic cohesion (China has very diverse ethnicities), and political stability. Internationally, the rise of China has inspired other emerging economies to become more confident. Furthermore, general economic prosperity in China has encouraged risk taking, which is the fuel that propels entrepreneurship, innovations, and productivity. Moreover, the seemingly single-minded focus on the build-out of infrastructure and education assures China's future competitive standing in the world. This having been said, China faces several challenges in allowing the yuan to rise to become the new hegemonic international currency.

First, the transition out of mercantilism will be a delicate one. Related to this is the "Triffin dilemma,"* which posits that the world's reserve currency needs to be issued by a country that runs large protracted current account deficits, in order to provide sufficient international currency for the world to use. It does not seem likely that China will start running persistent and large savings deficits any time soon.

Another key challenge is demographics. China's economic size may have just surpassed that of Japan, but China's per capita income is only one-tenth of Japan's. In 10 to 15 years, China is expected to hit a demographic turning point that is no less sharp than what Japan has experienced. This makes China at risk of getting old before it gets rich. Extrapolating from the experiences of the last decade without accounting for the powerful demographic headwind that China will face seems odd and uninformed.

I would also add that China faces yet another challenge: an ideological transition in policy. Capitalism rests on trust in

---

* This was an idea first proposed by economist Robert Triffin in the 1960s. He suggested that, for a country to supply enough of its currency for the rest of the world to hold, it will need to run persistent trade deficits to allow foreigners to "earn" the currency.

prices doing the work to equilibrate supply and demand, whereas communism distrusts prices and trusts quantity controls. While China may seem like a capitalist society on the surface, there are prevalent macroeconomic price controls. First, the price of money is controlled: China does not yet have a meaningful yield curve, as we've already mentioned. Interest rates are defined as the prices of money and liquidity, and they are still mostly preset in China.* Second, the prices of energy inputs are subsidized. Third, the price of the currency is distorted. In other words, three of the most important macroeconomic prices are controlled in China. For China to be able to develop a liquid and viable financial sector, it will have to somehow develop more trust in prices rather than quantity.

Bottom Line

From a multidecade perspective, the Chinese yuan, or an Asian currency unit that is centered on the yuan, will almost certainly become a major reserve and international currency one day. But for the yuan to supplant the dollar as the hegemonic reserve currency in the world *within the decade*, China will need to do everything right and the United States will need to do everything wrong. While the former seems likely, the latter is unlikely, at least within the decade.

In my opinion, the current debate between the yuan and the U.S. dollar is less about China versus the United States than is perhaps widely thought. It is also not a discussion about the dismal state—economically, politically, and perhaps militarily—in which the United States finds itself in this post–2008 era. Rather,

---

* Interest rates are the cost of borrowing, and therefore the "price" of money.

it is a debate about whether the Americans, as a people, still have the tenacity and the resilience to rise from the funk they are in. There is no debate on China's bright prospects in the foreseeable future. However, I contest a popular view that Americans are soft, confused, and no longer inspired. None of the problems in the United States is insurmountable. A short decade ago, the United States had great fiscal statistics; it is not clear to me that fiscal prudence and global competitiveness can never be restored in the United States. The United States still leads the world in innovation and higher education. All it takes, in my view, for debate about the dollar's hegemonic status as the world's currency to be put to bed is for the Americans to rediscover their hard Calvinist core.

CHAPTER 3

THE EURO: PAST, PRESENT, AND FUTURE[1]

Jörg Asmussen

"It is a big success. We have given European citizens a single currency, which is in line with what was promised: a currency which retains its value, which inspires confidence, a stable currency, at least as stable as the legacy currencies. Ten years ago, many believed this promise could not be fulfilled."
—Jean-Claude Trichet, European Central Bank President, January 2009

The Past: Setting the Course[2]

The European Economic and Monetary Union (EMU) and the single European currency are of historical significance for the economic and political development of Europe. The countries participating in the EMU brought their traditional national currencies together at the beginning of 1999 to form a common currency—the euro. By giving up their independent monetary policies, these states permanently ceded their existing national sovereignty over important aspects of policy to the supranational authority of the newly formed European Central Bank (ECB). This decision to forgo national sovereignty in favor of sovereignty at the supranational level was unprecedented in monetary history.

Initially, the integration of European monetary policy proceeded very slowly. This was largely due to the existence of the Bretton Woods fixed-exchange-rate system, which applied until the early 1970s, and controls on international capital flows, which were still being enforced in Europe at that time. From 1950 onward, international payment transactions in Europe were initially settled under the Organisation for European Economic Co-operation (OEEC) through the multilateral payments system of the European Payments Union (EPU). Toward the end of the 1950s, however, the system waned as several European countries made their currencies freely convertible.

With a growing level of international capital movements and mounting financial market integration came rising tensions in the international monetary system. This had an impact on the European Economic Community (EEC), established in 1957 by the Treaty of Rome. In the mid-1960s, the EEC members—of which there were six at that time—focused primarily on enhancing the exchange of information between national monetary authorities and intensifying efforts at cooperation among national governments, essentially by forming committees without decision-making powers. By the end of the 1960s, however, the need for more extensive cooperation was becoming obvious. Following up on a memorandum from the European Commission in February 1969 (referred to as the Barre Plan), a working party led by the then prime minister of Luxembourg, Pierre Werner, developed a plan to create the EMU. On the basis of this Werner Plan, the European Council took a decision of principle in March 1971 that the EMU was to be achieved progressively by 1980.

However, the 1971 dollar crisis, when the dollar's link to gold was severed amid concerns that the United States did not hold enough gold to redeem foreign-owned dollars, prevented the implementation of a formal resolution by the Council of Ministers of the European Communities (EC). Some countries, including the Federal Republic of Germany, temporarily abandoned the fixed link to the U.S. dollar and allowed their currencies to float freely. With the Washington monetary agreement of December 1971 (the Smithsonian Agreement), an attempt was made at an international level to restore stable exchange-rate parities. However, the disadvantage for the EC was that the general widening of the fluctuation margins against the U.S. dollar meant that exchange rates between EC currencies could fluctuate within an overall range of 9 percent. This widening of margins and its implications for the EC's agricultural policy, for instance, gave fresh impetus to efforts to create a special arrangement with narrower margins within the EC.

On March 21, 1972, the EC Council of Ministers adopted a resolution that was given concrete form through the Basel Accord and put in force on April 24, 1972. Among other things, it established the European "currency snake" and the European Monetary Cooperation Fund (EMCF). In the snake, the EC member states were to undertake to allow their currencies to fluctuate against one another within a range of only ±2.25 percent. The linked European currencies were able to move freely against other currencies, especially the U.S. dollar, which was floated in 1973.

Initial experience with the stabilization of intracommunity exchange rates showed that in the long term, a system of fixed exchange rates could work only between countries with sufficiently similar approaches to economic policy and a corresponding degree of economic convergence. In an appraisal dated April 1973, the European Commission concluded that only some of the envisaged progress toward integration had been made. In particular, the commission considered it necessary to transfer real economic policy powers to community bodies. The member states found this unacceptable, and a negative decision was made regarding starting the second stage of the EMU in line with the Werner Plan. Ultimately, the EMU project of that time failed because of fundamental differences of opinion regarding the objectives being pursued through the EMU and, in particular, because of the EC countries' unwillingness to subject themselves to a common stability objective. Consequently, their economic policy responses to the first oil crisis also diverged greatly.

The primary goal of the European Monetary System (EMS) was to strengthen monetary policy cooperation to create an area of monetary stability in Europe. The EMS helped to initiate far closer currency cooperation among member states, and in the 1980s, it also reinforced the growing willingness to see a closer convergence of economic and monetary policy among them. The EMS prompted most member states to gear their economic and monetary policies to developments in the most economically stable countries in the EC.

In June 1988, the European Council commissioned a working party to prepare for the EMU. The working party was chaired by Commission President Jacques Delors and included the EC central bank governors and three independent experts. It produced a report in April 1989 (referred to as the Delors Report) that proposed that the EMU be achieved in three stages. This project was approved by the European Council, which decided that the first stage of the EMU should begin on July 1, 1990, and that two intergovernmental conferences should be convened to prepare the amendments to the treaty, which were required in order to ensure that the further stages could be implemented. The outcome, after a year of discussion, was the Treaty on European Union, which was approved by the Heads of State and Government in Maastricht in December 1991. This Maastricht Treaty came into force on November 1, 1993, with the completion of national ratification procedures and formed the legal foundation for the further stages that were necessary to make the EMU a reality.

The First Stage

The first stage of the EMU was primarily concerned with gearing the national economic and monetary policies more closely to the requirements for monetary stability and budgetary discipline within the EC. This was to be achieved primarily by greater coordination of national economic and monetary policies.

The council decision on the attainment of progressive convergence in economic policies and performance during Stage 1 of the EMU introduced multilateral surveillance as a new coordination instrument for the community. This new innovative instrument covered all aspects of economic policy, both short and medium term, with particular emphasis on budgetary policy. In addition to the biannual surveillance procedures, the Council of Economic and Finance Ministers (Ecofin Council) was also able to make use of ad hoc consultations if economic developments within a member state or outside the community posed a risk to economic cohesion. The new coordination procedure was intended to initiate a learning process that would increasingly lead to compatible economic policies. The success of this process hinged crucially, however, on the willingness of the member states to comply. Apart from the freedom to publish its economic policy proposals and rulings, the council had no means of exerting pressure to make the member states subject their economic policy to the interests of Europe as a whole.

Another major innovation in the first stage of the EMU was the new approach to monetary policy cooperation. The tasks of the Committee of Governors established in 1964 were expanded by the Ecofin Council decision of March 12, 1990, on cooperation between the central banks of the member states of the EC. On the basis of a new mandate in which the objective of price stability was expressly given priority, the Committee of Governors was now able to express opinions to the national central banks on the orientation of monetary and exchange-rate policy, and also to express opinions to the Council of Ministers or individual governments. The Committee of Governors helped pave the way for the creation of the European Monetary Institute (EMI), established in the second stage of the EMU, which placed cooperation among the central banks on a new institutional footing.

The Second Stage

In keeping with the Maastricht Treaty, the second stage of the EMU began on January 1, 1994, and served to prepare for the transition to the final stage. This stage had two primary aims. The first was to create the legal, institutional, and organizational preconditions for the completion of the EMU in the third stage. The second was to intensify further the monitoring and coordination of economic policy so that a high degree of long-term convergence within the community could be achieved as a necessary prerequisite for entry into the final stage. Attention was focused on budgetary policy because the convergence criteria set out in the treaty could be met only if the member states followed a sound budgetary policy.

Pursuant to Article 121 of the EC Treaty, read in conjunction with the protocol on the convergence criteria referred to in Article 121 of the EC Treaty, a country's eligibility for joining the EMU was to be assessed using the following four criteria: (1) the member state has to demonstrate sustainable price stability, (2) the government's financial position, measured using the reference values set in the treaty, must be sustainable in the long term, (3) the member state must have participated in the exchange-rate mechanism of the EMS and have observed the normal margins without severe tensions and without devaluing for at least two years prior to the test, and (4) long-term interest rates may be no more than an average of two percentage points above the reference value of, at most, the three member states with the greatest price stability over a period of one year before the test.

The ban prohibiting central banks from lending to the public sector, which came into force at the start of the second stage, and governments' renunciation of privileged access to financial services institutions were likewise aimed at strengthening budgetary discipline. These provisions, which continued to apply after the introduction of the euro, ultimately forced the public sector to raise funds on market terms in the credit and capital markets. This was intended to strengthen budget discipline and thus eliminate a potential source of inflation.

In the second stage of the EMU, the economic policy of most EU member states was completely focused on meeting the convergence criteria laid down in the Maastricht Treaty. The pressure exerted on those member states that wished to participate under these criteria as entry requirements for the third stage, combined with the decision to enter the third stage on

January 1, 1999, led to a notable convergence of key economic data in most EU member states.

As a result of this development, and taking into account the EMI and European Commission convergence reports, the Ecofin Council determined on May 1, 1998, that, in its assessment, 11 member states (namely, Austria, Belgium, Finland, France, Germany, Ireland, Italy, Luxembourg, the Netherlands, Portugal, and Spain) met the preconditions for the introduction of the single currency. It recommended introducing the euro in these 11 countries on January 1, 1999. On the basis of this recommendation and of the European Parliament's opinion on the matter, the European Heads of State and Government confirmed the next day that the countries named in the recommendation met the necessary criteria for introducing the euro.

The Third Stage

On January 1, 1999, the euro became the common currency in the euro area, comprising the 11 member states that had qualified by meeting the convergence criteria. The start of the third stage of the EMU saw those 11 states pass their monetary sovereignty to the EC. The responsibility for the single monetary policy in the euro area was transferred to the ECB Council. On January 1, 2002, after the preparations for the cash changeover were complete, the euro was introduced physically in the form of euro-denominated banknotes and euro- and cent-denominated coins.

The Present: Benefits and Reforms

A euro crisis?

Today, at least 10 years after euro notes and coins were first introduced in the euro countries, it is fair to say that the euro has lived up to its proponents' expectations. Inflation is low, the currency is strong, and the euro's role as one of the world's most prominent reserve currencies is increasing.

Stable Inflation Rate at a Low Level

The euro has ensured internal price stability. De Grauwe (2008) argues that the "inflation record in the euro zone has been outstanding," even during crisis years. Since the foundation of the EMU, the annual inflation rate within the euro zone has remained within the ECB's target framework of 2 percent on average. The euro "has provided price stability to previously inflation-prone countries" (Pisani-Ferry and Sapir, 2009). Even in Germany, inflation rates have so far been lower than at the time of the deutsche mark. Since 1999, inflation in Germany (at 1.5 percent per annum) has, on average, been lower than it was during the last three decades of the deutsche mark era (when it stood at 3 percent per annum; see Figure 3-1). The

Figure 3-1 Price Development in Germany Before and After the Introduction of the Euro

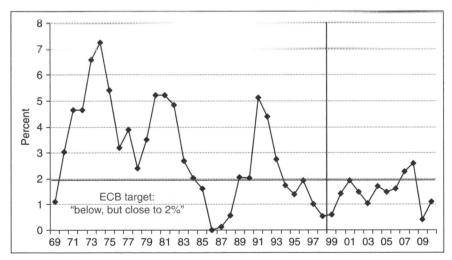

Source: Federal Statistical Office of Germany

euro also compares favorably against the U.S. dollar. While the eurozone inflation rate from 1999 to 2010 averaged 2 percent, inflation in the United States ran at 2.4 percent over the same period. In other words, over the course of just one decade, the U.S. dollar has lost about 20 percent of its purchasing power in comparison with the euro.

Stable Exchange Rate and Reserve Currency

Although the external value of a currency is not a value per se, it is important for psychological reasons. In scenarios in which a currency's price is decreasing against the prices of other major currencies, analysts immediately fear capital flight and a loss of trust. The euro is also doing very well in this regard and has ensured external price stability. When it was introduced as an accounting currency, it was worth only US$1.18, and when euro notes and coins were physically introduced, its value even lay below parity with the U.S. dollar. Since then, the euro has traded at well above that rate (see Figure 3-2). The euro has also held up in comparison with the deutsche mark. The latter reached its all-time high against the U.S. dollar in May 1995 (when it was worth US$0.74, which was approximately the same as the exchange rate between the dollar and the euro in early 2012).

The euro has established itself as one of the world's leading reserve currencies, surpassed only by the U.S. dollar (see Figure 3-3). While other internationally important currencies, such as the U.S. dollar and the yen, have seen their share of global currency reserves shrink, the percentage held in euros has continuously grown, from just under 18 percent in 1999 to around 26 percent in December 2010.[3]

Figure 3-2 ECB Reference Exchange Rate, U.S. Dollar to Euro

Source: ECB

Figure 3-3 Composition of Foreign Exchange Reserves (Average for 2001–2010)

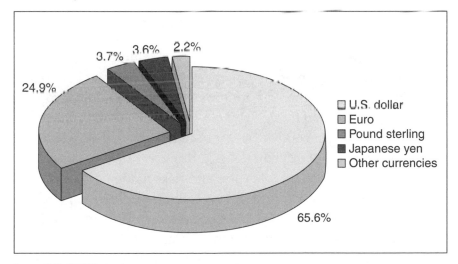

Source: IMF COFER database

Benefits of the Euro

The countries of the euro zone benefit considerably from the fact that the "euro is as stable and credible as the best-performing currencies previously used in the euro area countries" (ECB, 2011). There is widespread agreement among experts that eurozone countries draw more benefits from the euro than they drew from strong and stable national currencies. These benefits go well beyond price and exchange-rate stability.

Studies on the EMU's effect on trade yield different outcomes in terms of numbers; while using different methodologies, they still all suggest that the EMU has had a positive effect: "[T]he effect of EMU on bilateral trade between member countries ranges between 5 and 10 percent, when compared to trade between all other pairs of countries, and between 9 and 20 percent, when compared to trade among non-EMU countries" (Micco, Stein, and Ordoñez, 2003). One major reason for this is that considerable savings are realized every year by companies trading within the eurozone. The introduction of the euro eliminated foreign exchange transaction costs resulting from (1) buying and selling foreign currencies on the foreign exchange markets, (2) protecting oneself against adverse exchange-rate movements, (3) making cross-border payments in foreign currencies, which entail high fees, and (4) keeping several currency accounts that make account management more difficult (ECB, 2011).

In the past, exchange-rate costs and risks hindered trade and competition across borders. The euro eliminated exchange-rate fluctuations and, therefore, foreign exchange risks within the euro zone, thus facilitating business planning and increasing cross-border investments. Experts estimate that the average positive effect of the euro on aggregate foreign direct investment

(FDI) flows within the euro area is about 15 percent, while its impact on FDI flows from outside the euro area is about 7 percent (Mongelli and Wyplosz, 2009). Consumers naturally benefit from the euro as well because it facilitates price comparisons, thereby increasing competition and lowering prices. The single currency also gives tourism a significant boost because it makes traveling across European countries much easier.

Besides its economic benefits, the common currency is of inestimable political value. The euro is the most far-ranging result of and commitment to European integration—it is both a symbol of and a driving force behind that integration. According to research into public opinion, the euro is the most frequently mentioned EU symbol in the eurozone countries. When asked to say what the EU means to them personally, one out of two citizens in the euro area mentioned the euro, outranking "peace" and the "freedom to travel, study and work" (European Commission, 2010).

Sovereign Debt Crisis

The crisis, which began in 2010 in Greece, indicates that although the euro has been in good shape, the same cannot be said for all of the countries in the eurozone. Some of them have been severely affected by the sovereign debt crisis and face a high level of indebtedness—Greece has a debt-to-GDP ratio of 157.7 percent, Ireland 112 percent, and Portugal 101.7 percent (European Commission, 2011). The reasons are manifold. The sequence of serious crises has naturally placed a special burden on public budgets as a result of the emergency and economic stimulus packages that had to be introduced. However, the euro countries that are most indebted today are the ones that have too long pursued the wrong budgetary and fiscal

Figure 3-4 10-Year Bond Spreads Compared to German Bonds

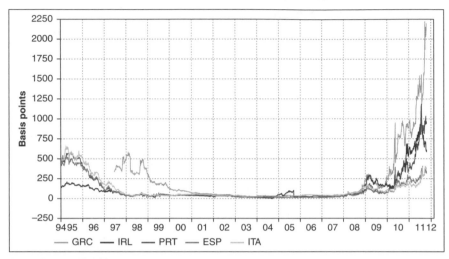

Source: Reuters EcoWin

policies while lacking competitiveness. A stunning market failure has made the situation still worse. Since the introduction of the euro, bond markets have not punished unsound fiscal and economic policies early enough. For a decade, the interest rates for euro countries were converging, although the countries' national fiscal and economic policies diverged considerably (see Figure 3-4). The markets did not evaluate risks appropriately and exert discipline. They became increasingly risk-averse during the crisis, however, fueling it as a result.

EMU Reform

The eurozone is currently under particular strain because the global debt crisis and the financial difficulties of some member states have revealed the weaknesses of the EMU.

All of the weaknesses that were exposed during the debt crisis led to a loss of market confidence in the entire eurozone.

In order to regain this confidence, the European governments have to address these deficiencies. The Heads of State and Government of the eurozone and their finance ministers have already taken crucial decisions in this regard that will lead to a comprehensive reform of the current rules and architecture of the EMU:

1. *Strengthening budgetary surveillance.* One of the most important decisions has been to strengthen the supranational surveillance mechanism for national budgetary policies within the framework of the Stability and Growth Pact (SGP), an agreement adopted in 1997 to enforce budget discipline among nations that use the euro.
    - As often discussed by experts, this was achieved "to take better account of the debt criterion" of the pact (Le Cacheux and Touya, 2007). Debt reduction will be mandatory for every member country of the eurozone. Up until now, it was possible to initiate an "excessive deficit procedure" against a eurozone country only if its government deficit was too great, that is, more than 3 percent of GDP. In the future, the European Commission will also be able to launch the procedure:
        - If a balanced or almost balanced budget is not achieved in the medium term.
        - If a country's total debt is too large. In the future, member states with a debt-to-GDP ratio of more than 60 percent will be required to reduce the amount of excess by one-twentieth a year until their debt amounts to only 60 percent of GDP.
    - Sanctions will become effective earlier. With the new obligation to have a balanced or nearly balanced budget

in the medium term, sanctions will be part of the "preventive arm" of the SGP, that is, they will apply even if the general government deficit is not more than 3 percent of GDP. If the necessary corrective fiscal policy measures are not applied adequately, a country will have to make an interest-bearing deposit amounting to 0.2 percent of GDP, which could, in further steps, be transformed into a non-interest-bearing deposit and eventually into a monetary penalty. Sanctions as part of the "corrective arm" of the SGP will now take effect more quickly as well, that is, when the government deficit is already larger than 3 percent of GDP and/or when overall debt is not being reduced adequately.

- Sanctions will be increasingly automatic. In the past, it was too easy to block sanctions, and the European Commission was unable to defend the SGP against the national interests of the member states (Heipertz and Verdun, 2010). This deficit has been adjusted significantly. In the future, sanctions will automatically apply unless a large majority in the council halts the process (by means of a "reverse majority").
- Sanctions will become more comprehensive. In the medium term, it will be possible not only to impose fiscal and monetary penalties, but to deny EU resources to a member state on a greater scale than has currently been the case. Payments from certain EU funds are to be tied to sustainable fiscal policies.

2. *Strengthening macroeconomic coordination and surveillance.* European governments have reacted to experts' warning that "the current institutional framework [of the EMU] for cooperation is not enough to avoid the accumulation of imbalances" within the eurozone (Ortiz Martínez, 2009).

With the newly agreed-upon Euro Plus Pact, European governments are showing that from now on, they are resolved to coordinate their economic policies and to concentrate on improving the competitiveness of their countries and of Europe as a whole. From this point onward, the countries participating in the pact will agree each year on common objectives, which will then entail concrete national commitments. While the pact is first and foremost meant to foster the competitiveness of all member states and to address macroeconomic imbalances; it is meant to strengthen the long-term sustainability of public finances by, among other things, anchoring a debt brake in national laws or constitutions, adapting the pension systems to national demographics, and placing a limit on early retirement schemes. With the introduction of a new procedure for macroeconomic surveillance, an alert mechanism will monitor the measures under the Euro Plus Pact in order to detect, prevent, and, if necessary, correct excessive macroeconomic imbalances. Both budgetary and macroeconomic surveillance will, in the future, be coordinated and intensified within a European planning and reporting cycle called the European semester.

3. *Strengthening the surveillance and regulation of financial markets.* As "[t]here is an emerging consensus on the need to strengthen cooperation between the supervisory authorities responsible for major cross-border institutions and to promote a more convergent and consistent application of regulations" (Papademos, 2009), European governments have established a new European system of financial supervision, the European Financial Stability Facility (EFSF), to make the financial sector sounder and

more resilient. The newly created European Systemic Risk Board (ESRB) will monitor the stability of the financial system as a whole, warn about impending systemic risks, and issue recommendations on how to eliminate those risks. Three new European supervisory authorities in the fields of banking, insurance, and securities will work together with national supervisory authorities in the surveillance of institutions and markets. Various measures have been put in place to strengthen financial institutions, of which the Basel III international bank capital rules are of particular importance because they force financial institutions to maintain more and higher-quality capital buffers. Member states are also called upon to introduce instruments and procedures for restructuring failing banks, the collapse of which would pose a systemic risk to the banking sector. Recapitalization should preferably take place via the private sector, with supplementary capital being provided by governments if necessary.

4. *Establishing an institutional emergency and crisis management mechanism.* All of these measures will make it quite unlikely that the euro countries will face financial problems in the future that are on a par with those seen in recent years. However, if, despite all of these precautionary measures, another sovereign debt crisis does occur in the EU, a robust institutional crisis management mechanism will be in place thanks to the establishment of the European Stability Mechanism (ESM), which will replace the existing temporary EFSF in July 2013. This new institution will be well equipped to assist countries whose illiquidity threatens the stability of the eurozone as a whole. The ESM's toolbox will consist

of loans (provided on condition of strict economic reform and adjustment programs), the right to intervene in primary and secondary markets, the ability to recapitalize financial institutions of systemic importance, and precautionary programs. It will also have clear rules and mechanisms for worst-case scenarios, namely, a euro country's *insolvency*.

Most experts argue, "[t]he Greek crisis demonstrates the inadequate macroeconomic crisis management framework in the EU and the need to establish a more orderly sovereign debt restructuring process" (Kern, 2011). This is exactly what European governments have taken care of with the construction of the new stability mechanism. The ESM will allow for orderly restructuring in the event of insolvency by regulating *when* debt restructuring becomes necessary and by choosing *which* procedure is needed. Standardized debt restructuring clauses (collective action clauses, introduced in all new sovereign bond contracts of the eurozone issued for a period of more than one year) will assist in fostering an early dialogue between the debtor and the bondholders, as well as prevent individual creditors from blocking negotiations on specific debt restructuring models.

The eurozone is facing serious problems. Achieving reform in Greece, Ireland, and Portugal, while at the same time preventing contagion from spreading to other eurozone countries, is a challenge of tremendous proportions. However, there is no reason to have doubts of its success because European governments have agreed on a comprehensive set of measures to address the institutional shortcomings of the eurozone's past. If they are successful in implementing these measures effectively, the euro and the eurozone will have a bright future—a future within a multipolar currency system.

The Future: A Stable Multipolar Currency System

The financial crisis has placed a massive burden on our economies, and several countries continue to face huge challenges in terms of putting their houses back in order. It has now become clear that past growth dynamics in the world economy and its regional subsystems, including the euro area and the EU, were not always based on sound economic fundamentals. Especially in the run-up to the financial crisis, the growth dynamics in advanced countries were distorted by unsound leverage in private- and public-sector balance sheets. At the global level, uneven macroeconomic policies and exchange-rate regimes led to the buildup of significant macroeconomic imbalances. The persistence of these imbalances, giving rise to instabilities in the global financial system, has been one of the motivations for the G-20 to place the reform of the international monetary system at the top of the international agenda. Europe has actively supported this policy focus and has an ongoing, strategic interest in being part of the process of shaping a new international monetary and financial order.

The international monetary system is currently still largely focused on the U.S. dollar as the dominant international reserve currency. While the sustainability of the "twin deficits" in the United States and exchange-rate policy in key emerging markets have been the subject of debate for a long time, adjustment so far has been slow. Despite some hope of renewed resilience in growth and adjustment, the risks of crises are still looming. Along with the substantial increase in international capital flows over the last 20 years, balance of payments crises have grown significantly, too. Although the focus is currently on Europe, and on the peripherals in the eurozone in particular, the sovereign debt crisis has also reached the United States. Eichengreen (2005) has argued that the dominance of the U.S. dollar as an international reserve currency is not insulated from the risk of a sharp reversal, especially if the U.S. current account deficit and fiscal position are not brought to more sustainable levels. For a long time, a key issue has therefore been how the international monetary system can be reformed to avoid the rise of global imbalances and make the system more stable and resilient.

First, we should evaluate whether the euro can close ranks further with the U.S. dollar as an international reserve currency. To answer this question, it is useful to start by examining some of the fundamental preconditions for a currency to secure the status of an international reserve currency.

Preconditions for Reserve Currency Status

According to Lim (2006), there are five factors that facilitate international currency status: large economic size, the existence of a well developed financial system, confidence in the currency's value, political stability, and network externalities. Additional features of the current international monetary system and requirements for currencies to assume reserve status are large-scale current and financial account convertibility, a high degree of capital mobility, surveillance of economic policies, and cooperation on monetary policy making at regional or multilateral levels (Bénassy-Quéré and Pisani-Ferry, 2011).

To date, the U.S. dollar has dominated the international scene on account of its fulfilling almost all of these criteria. Yet, when viewed historically, the U.S. dollar's assumption of its current dominant reserve currency status was the outcome of a gradual process of overtaking the pound sterling between the two World Wars. Despite the difference in terms of economic, political, and military power, the reserve status of the pound sterling had succeeded in outpacing that of the dollar for many years beforehand, with the primary reason being network externalities, particularly large demand-side and supply-side economies of scale. This is explained by the fact that with larger and more frequent use of the pound sterling worldwide, transaction costs decreased, and the individual utility of trade in terms of this currency increased. Inherent network externalities produced a situation of inertia, which helped the pound sterling to remain in its dominant position longer than the fundamentals would have indicated. Once the U.S. dollar assumed reserve currency status, it built network externalities of its own.

The hegemonic dominance of the U.S. dollar in the international monetary system has remained mostly undisputed in the years since the abolition of the Bretton Woods system. The unparalleled stable and liquid market in the United States means that the U.S. dollar has remained the currency of choice. Based on the historical experience of the relationship between the pound sterling and the U.S. dollar, however, the dominant role of the dollar as the key international reserve will not necessarily remain unchallenged. Future shifts between evolving new reserve currencies and the U.S. dollar are possible. Eichengreen and Flandreau (2009) showed that despite network externalities and the inertia of a dominant currency (the pound sterling), the U.S. dollar was able to become the world's leading currency in just one decade.

The main challenge facing the euro, the yuan, and other emerging-market currencies in becoming international reserve currencies is developing deeper domestic financial markets through which positive network externalities and a wider use of reserves in private-sector transactions can arise. In the current

G-20 process, work is being undertaken on the deepening of local currency bond markets and the improved management of volatile global capital flows. Especially for those emerging-market economies that wish to enhance the absorption of capital flows, the focus will, therefore, have to be placed on ensuring the robustness of their domestic financial institutional setting (Prasad, 2011).

Current Trends in the Reserve Status of the Euro and the U.S. Dollar

The transition to a multipolar currency system is already well on its way. The euro has made its mark on the international financial system. While the euro has gained only slightly in terms of banks' international assets (see Figure 3-5), the share

Figure 3-5 Banks' Foreign Currency Assets and Outstanding International Bonds and Notes

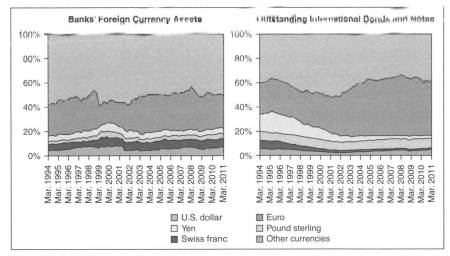

Source: Bank for International Settlements

of euro-denominated international bonds outstanding has risen from 25 percent in 1993 to more than 45 percent in 2011.

U.S. monetary policy can still have a potentially large impact on foreign private and official market participants' investment choices, thus influencing global wealth and liquidity (IMF, 2011a). The ongoing importance of the United States as a global financial investment destination can be seen when comparing U.S. dollar asset holdings. While foreign banks hold some US$5,400 billion of assets in the United States, U.S. banks hold only assets worth US$2,500 billion abroad, which is the largest net investment position difference in the world, according to IMF spillover analysis (IMF, 2011b). This means that the U.S. dollar retains a strong position in international finance.

Can the U.S. Dollar Be Challenged?

Some economists argue that despite the existence of an international financial market that has grown enormously and decreased transaction costs, positive network externalities are still working to the benefit of the dominant currency today (Meissner and Oomes, 2008). Some take the argument further, stating that the optimum would be to have just one international main reserve currency (McKinnon, 2005). It is, however, far from clear whether any multipolar currency system will finally converge toward unipolarity. Eichengreen and Flandreau (2009) argue that several currencies were already in use to varying extents as international reserve currencies before World War I (namely, the pound sterling, the French franc, and the German mark) as well as between the wars (the pound sterling and the U.S. dollar). Furthermore, today's global market is sufficiently liquid and transaction costs are low, which means that multiple currencies can reach the scale necessary for network externalities to have an effect. As Mateos y Lago and colleagues (2010) outline, alternative currencies—fully substitutable for the U.S. dollar—could "overcome the network externalities that strongly push all actors to converge to a dominant currency."

Is There a Role for the Special Drawing Right?

The Special Drawing Right (SDR) was created in 1969 by the International Monetary Fund to support the Bretton Woods fixed-exchange-rate system as a supplementary reserve asset (IMF, 2012). Its role since then has, however, been limited. Yet the debate among academic economists continues to focus on the question of whether the SDR could become a true international reserve asset and a possible substitute for the U.S. dollar or gold to support the expansion of world trade and financial development. Most recently, the question of the future role of the SDR has been taken up by the G-20 in the context of work on the reform of the international monetary system in the run-up to G-20 summits. While strengthening the SDR is a long-term process, progress has been made in exploring a criteria-based path under which the SDR basket of currencies at the IMF could be broadened, in particular with regard to the possible inclusion of the yuan. Technical as this may seem, it may prove to be another step toward a multipolar currency system. The G-20 working group on reforming the international monetary system has emphasized that this process would contribute to the internationalization of currencies as a market-driven process, and that the process would also imply countries increasing their degree of exchange-rate flexibility and relying less on capital control measures, moving toward a more liberalized flow of capital into and out of countries.

The potential role of the SDR should not, however, be over-estimated. The stability of the international monetary system depends primarily on strengthening macroeconomic policies, economic governance, financial regulation, and supervisory frameworks at the level of the respective currency areas and countries. This is necessary in order to reduce and prevent a renewed buildup of global imbalances. It remains to be seen to what extent an enhanced role for the SDR could complement these tasks.

Sustaining the Euro as a Key Player in the Multipolar Currency System

Europe has a strategic interest in supporting an emerging multipolar currency system in which there are multiple reserve currencies. The underlying shift toward a multipolar system is reinforced by the present trend, in which major central banks may wish to hold a more diversified portfolio of multiple reserve currencies (Ghosh, Ostry, and Tsangarides, 2010). The diversification of reserve assets may be induced by different factors, namely, the availability of high-quality assets, liquidity and size of the market, network effects, trade patterns, and the currency denomination of trade. Ghosh, Ostry, and Tsangarides (2010) argue that central banks "will want to diversify risk in order to preserve the 'real value' of their reserve portfolios." Indeed, the share of the euro in global currency reserves has increased constantly (see Figure 3-6). In terms of the composition of foreign exchange reserves, the euro is already an important anchor currency for many Eastern European and African economies (Lim, 2006).

Sharing the responsibility for providing the main currencies among different countries and regions should help to

Figure 3-6   Share of Global Currency Reserves

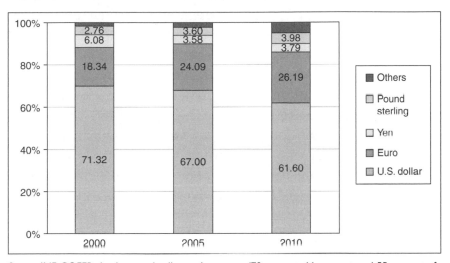

Source: IMF COFER database; only allocated reserves (78 percent, 66 percent, and 55 percent of total global reserves, respectively)

increase the stability of the international monetary system (World Bank, 2011) The supply of liquidity by different cen tral banks and the augmented supply and diversity of global traded assets should improve capital allocation and risk shar- ing, thus enhancing the system's resilience to (idiosyncratic) shocks. Having more international main currencies in use should also help to increase the legitimacy of the international monetary system by having a fair distribution of costs and benefits and creating a widening of international cooperation, which would reduce the risks of protectionism and competi- tive devaluations (or "currency wars").

However, the future of the euro and its contribution to the stability of the international monetary system will primarily be assessed against economic performance in the euro area itself, namely, the euro area's success in safeguarding financial

stability and augmenting potential growth, reforming entitle-
ment systems, and meeting the demographic challenge, as well
as in fostering the efficiency and openness of capital markets
and the stability of the exchange rate.

Despite the euro area's current challenges in dealing with
sovereign debt and competitiveness issues, there are grounds
for optimism. The euro's positive role in accompanying a transition toward a multipolar currency system can be illustrated
by the large external position of the euro area in terms of its
share of world trade and the rise of net foreign capital inflows
(see Figure 3-7). Even before the formal adoption of the euro,
a steady increase in the inflow of foreign direct investment
(FDI) into the euro area (and its predecessor countries) can be
observed from 1989 onward, capped by two positive outliers
in 2000 and 2007. A similar development can be observed for
portfolio investments (see Figure 3-8), the trend being broken

Figure 3-7 Net Foreign Capital Inflows into the Euro Area

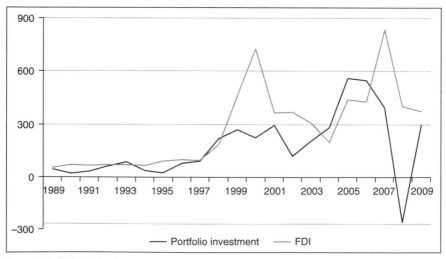

Source: World Bank database

Figure 3-8 Market Capitalization of Listed Companies

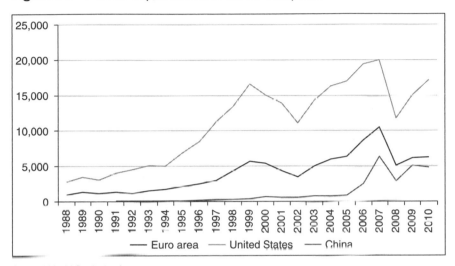

Source: World Bank database

only by a sharp decrease during the recent financial crisis. In fact, when the euro was introduced in 1999, there were shifts in official investors' foreign exchange holdings (Lim, 2006).

The Next 20 Years

The enormous market size and financial depth of the euro area are properties that make the euro a credible candidate for an increased international role. Despite its more moderate outlook in terms of demographic developments, the dimensions of the euro area can still be expected to grow with the entry of new countries into the common currency area (Eichengreen, 2009). Low and stable levels of inflation, credible government policies, and open and deep financial markets will pave the way for the euro to remain a strong global reserve currency. The consequent response to the current crisis is to strengthen policy fundamentals and stability,

119

as well as to foster further economic and financial integration in the single European market.

Furthermore, the euro's reserve role, as well as its policies, will help other nations integrate into a multipolar reserve system. For instance, going forward, the rise of emerging-market economies, especially Brazil, India, and China, will continue in a dynamic manner. In 2020–2030, many more financial and trade transactions will be conducted in the currencies of these countries, serving as a benchmark for the growth of the real economies in emerging markets. Concerns over volatility in capital flows and a cost-benefit analysis of artificially lowering the value of their currencies will perhaps be reassessed more neutrally. The cost to China of not allowing the yuan to appreciate is financial repression and a continuously closed capital account. As Prasad (2011) indicates, current account balances may, in the future, be dominated less by trade flows and more by net factor income flows and their effects on the capital account. Both for the U.S. dollar and for the euro, this means that securing policy credibility on the basis of strong economic fundamentals will become much more important.

For the time being, advanced countries are still much more financially integrated into the global economy than emerging-market economies. Prasad (2011) explains that the median level of the ratio of gross stocks of external assets and liabilities to GDP more than doubled over the last decade in advanced economies; but the ratio is also on the rise for Brazil, India, China, and Russia. The main point here is that after the financial crisis, the world will still be dominated by increased global financial integration. And this crisis has shown that financial spillovers can carry risks around the globe.

Given these trends, global cooperation and policy coordination are key factors. It could be argued that the main advantage of a more multipolar currency system is that it contributes to enhancing policy discipline among the reserve-issuing countries in the form of peer pressure that arises from potential substitutability (IMF, 2010). With credible alternatives to the U.S. dollar as an international reserve asset, issuers "will feel market discipline earlier and more consistently" (Eichengreen, 2011). Such a possible gain in stability in terms of major currencies could also lead to lower global reserve holdings. Furthermore, the current incongruence in the system that leads to the building up of enormous precautionary reserves can be overcome by a more multipolar system because currencies would be held primarily for transaction purposes (Mateos y Lago et al., 2009).

Conclusion

For the euro area, the key question is whether it can put its house back in order and assimilate the divergent economies into a zone of stability. At the same time, the euro area must succeed in inducing a renewed impetus for integration with more competitive, closely linked markets, especially where financial services are concerned (Lim, 2006). The euro can reinforce its role as a global reserve currency only once the euro area succeeds in reestablishing policy credibility. In order to secure this role, the euro area must advance with a much deeper degree of fiscal integration and solve the questions of its governance by means of more political integration. In the end, domestic factors will determine whether the euro will be a successful international reserve currency, shaped by the success of fiscal consolidation, structural reforms, and monetary policy making by the ECB (Prati and Schinasi, 1997).

The benefits from further economic and financial integration are still substantial. Despite the current challenges facing the euro area, the IMF has also been upbeat in stating that "executing the structural reform agenda with more emphasis on ensuring contestability and competition will greatly bolster growth prospects" for the euro area (IMF, 2011c).

There has not been consensus on an overall concept of how to repair the damage done by the crisis in a way that creates a sound and stable international monetary system in the future. The G-20's close cooperation on policy during the crisis and beyond will not remain an exception; global superpowers will need to continue to work closely together. A challenge will be to address the medium- to long-term issues. Sovereign debt problems in some countries in the euro area have been looming for too long, as has now become clear. At this current juncture, public policy is still preoccupied with the immediate management of the fallout from the crisis. Nonetheless, the next decade will be decisive because major changes will come to the fore—especially in terms of the further rise of emerging markets and their financial systems and currencies.

The reform of the international monetary system is not just an issue for a single G-20 summit, but one of the strategic issues for the next 20 years. Instabilities in the current system are not disputed. The move toward a multipolar currency system is well founded for economic reasons and will foster international financial stability. It is a long-term challenge. The fallout from the present crisis has reminded us of the underlying currents in the global economy that have been far from sound. These risks justify a reevaluation of past trends in the international monetary system as we move ahead. The euro can lead the way to reform if Europe is ready to assume a key leadership role internationally and if

Europe is able to establish a consensus in terms of reforming and strengthening its governance further internally.

The objectives and plans for European integration, shaped by differing national traditions and experiences, have often varied considerably over the last 50 years, both among nations and within individual countries. And to some extent they still do—despite all of the efforts and progress made in integration. On the one hand, this diverse range of objectives is part of Europe's cultural wealth. On the other hand, this diversity sometimes impedes the commonality needed to achieve the objective of the process of integration. This is especially true when trying to develop and implement joint ideas for specific political objectives, action plans, and essential institutional structures, which are particularly important in a permanent currency union.

In spite of all the advantages and benefits for all of us, there is the danger that because of the almost permanent state of crisis, Europe's citizens may lose confidence in Europe and the euro. Therefore, answers to fundamental questions are needed. The euro area today is faced with a fundamental political dilemma: we cannot simultaneously pursue the three goals of democracy, national self-determination, and economic integration. We must opt for two of these three things, or at least place them in a clearly defined relationship (see also Rodrik, 2011).

Today's basic consensus on monetary policy is the result of a long and, at times, very painful learning process that has also often created critical situations. But the benefit of hindsight also shows that most of the currency-related crises were caused largely by inconsistent or completely incompatible national policies. Overcoming them, however, has also often led to the discovery of new approaches and ways forward that have largely advanced political and economic integration in Europe. That is because, as a rule, crises offer potential for new progress as well—at least if the correct conclusions are drawn from them.

In view of the process of globalization, and faced with emerging powers such as China, India, and Brazil, European countries will be able to exert influence at the global level only if they act together. Wall (2008) argues that the "future is too unpredictable to say with confidence that this will be the Asian century. What is sure, however, is that we will be part of a multi-polar world and there is no single European country that can, by itself, constitute one of the poles. Only Europe united, politically and economically, can do so. And that is impossible while we run our economic and fiscal policies on the present national bases." Clearly, we need further bold steps to improve the governance of the euro area as a whole.

CHAPTER 4

WHAT HISTORY TELLS US ABOUT THE EURO'S FUTURE

John Taylor

"What we should grasp, however, from the lessons of European history is that, first, there is nothing necessarily benevolent about programmes of European integration; second, the desire to achieve grand utopian plans often poses a grave threat to freedom; and third, European unity has been tried before, and the outcome was far from happy."
—Margaret Thatcher, Stagecraft, 2002

In the last few decades, more than a few fashionable writers have followed the lead of Francis Fukuyama in *The End of History and the Last Man* (1992), treating his thesis as a given and implying that the world has advanced—or at least changed—so much that any analysis of previous historical events and relationships is a waste of time. Accordingly, if any research were to be carried out, the hypotheses generated from it would only lead to erroneous conclusions.

Although Fukuyama's concept has been challenged by many mainstream political and social historians, his "end of history" attitude seems to have become the dominant paradigm for the financial world. And, even if this paradigm isn't often stated, the impression is that the world of finance has changed so much that any inferences drawn from the past have to be treated with great care. Putting it bluntly, if a market event occurred before the end of World War II, it doesn't count; ignore it. Analyses of prices, earnings, yield curves, credit spreads, and how these relate to and interact with the underlying economy or political events almost always start with the end of the war.

Those economists and economic historians who look at the whole span of history and draw modern conclusions from them have been few and far between. Notable among them were Charles Kindleberger (*Mania, Panics, and Crashes*, 1978) and Hyman Minsky (*Stabilizing an Unstable Economy*, 1986). Although many great minds have studied the Depression era, including Milton Friedman, Anna Schwartz, and Ben Bernanke, it could be argued that their analyses and conclusions were rooted in that time and have not been as effectively applied to the problems of today. The work on the Depression actually seems to illuminate the differences between the prewar system and that of today, rather than helping to unearth new similarities that would allow us to manage current failings. Perhaps Kindleberger and Minsky's success in analyzing the whole of economic time, resulting in a deeper understanding of today's issues, is a sign that the study of the capitalist system's repeated failings would be a more effective way to pinpoint and analyze the universal— including the modern—qualities of that system.

When analyzing currency movements and valuations, the division between significance and not-worth-looking-at is even more rigidly demarcated. The date when history begins is late February 1973, when the last vestige of the Bretton Woods system was finally swept away and floating rates began. Reading modern currency analysis, one would be convinced that history began less than 40 years ago. Before that, the world was dark and primeval. I am not aware of any recent (post–1990) academic or serious institutional studies that attempt to tie currency movements in the Bretton Woods era or the pre–World War II era with modern currency issues. The chasm is so wide that the data we use to dissect the markets and their movements today were not even available during the Bretton Woods period, as we now approach the analytical process so differently from the way we did back then. The data that we so love to load into computer systems and pore over for hours either were discarded in the trash or did not even exist back then.

Focusing on the mountain of data that describes the currency markets and relationships over the last decade or two and ignoring the past because it cannot be sliced and diced the way that our modern machinery allows is a major blind spot that has led today's investors, traders, and government authorities to pursue ill-chosen paths. We must see currency relationships as part of the ongoing political interplay among countries, something that has not changed dramatically in the past 300 or 400 years.

To think of currencies in this way, we must understand financial markets as being more than the modern places where we raise capital, invest, and transact business on a day-to-day or year-to-year basis. Markets do not actually depend on capitalism, as they have underpinned civilization from the very beginning. They can be seen as nothing less than the monetary and transaction-based expression of the underlying social and political structure. Feudal markets were very different from the markets of the Roman Empire, and markets can be thought of as a good way to quantitatively measure the reality of the society as a whole—how it actually functions and how well it may be doing at any given time. The foreign exchange market is a particular subset of markets, as it measures the relationship among coherent social systems organized into nation-states.

In the past 200 years, capitalism and the Industrial Revolution brought markets to the forefront, sharpening their relationship to the average person and developing a more structurally intact process for global trade and exchange. The intersocietal measures of valuation and credit quality or trust have developed as the global system has grown and changed, but the basics are unaltered—can I trade with that country; if I invest there, will I make a decent return; and will I get my money back?

As the foreign exchange valuation of an individual country, and the rate of change of that valuation in relation to its trading partners, is an integral part of the economic and social fabric of each of the countries involved, one must consider and understand much more than the week-to-week, or even year-to-year, movements in the currency market to divine how the currencies will move in the very long term. Considering that the currency markets have been floating for 39 years as this is being written and that the Bretton Woods system controlled the currency markets for only 25 years before collapsing, the post–World War II experience does not really tell us much about the long-term nature of the foreign exchange market and in what direction it might be moving.

Between 1914 and 1946, gold was accepted as the measure by which currency relationships between countries would be managed, but so many crises intervened that individual countries suffered inflation, deflation, overheated growth, or depression depending on their relationship to gold—were they tied to it or not? Although moving into and out of a tight relation with gold allowed countries to manipulate their economies, the gold standard could not overcome other social and economic problems that prevented it from fostering the development of a stable global economy. Many people believe that gold was much more successful in the 44 years prior to World War I. At that time, the gold exchange standard coexisted with strong global trade growth and the aggressive European and North American expansion of manufacturing. Four systems in 142 years! The one thing we can say is that we have no stable system and the future is uncertain.

Europe's unsettled position influences two interrelated currency dilemmas that are troubling our current floating-rate system at this time. The turmoil within Europe will shift the balance of global power away from that continent for the next few decades, but by itself it should not cause undue disruption in the floating-rate system of the past 39 years. However, it should dramatically alter the relative values among currencies and could affect the choice of the reserve currency or the reserve system itself.

The political hubris that led to the construction of a unified currency, a system far more constricting than the gold exchange system, must lead either to the creation of a unified European state, a process that is likely to span many decades, or to the destruction of the European Union and the renewed fragmentation of Europe. This feeds the second dilemma, one that we have seen before: as global reserve structures are inherently unstable, what happens as Europe's collapse hastens the West's loss of its dominant status?

The currency hegemon, England in the late nineteenth and early twentieth centuries, and the United States since 1946, seems to become increasingly enfeebled as a result of its reserve status. Because the monetary stance of the dominant reserve country defines the tightness or looseness of money throughout the world, money, once created, runs from its domestic banking system to the most profitable investment arenas around the world. Throughout the twentieth century, this drew money away from the reserve country, but now, since the start of the twenty-first century, this move has become an exaggerated sucking process, as the hegemon is forced to run a too-loose policy no matter what its own internal system might demand, since the world economy depends on the dollars it prints.

For decades on end, the United States has been the source of global liquidity just to keep its own economy moving along. As a consequence of the resulting tendency toward dollar weakness, over the past few decades, the global reserve responsibility has been expanding to other currencies, most recently the euro, which has become the secondary reserve currency (see Figure 4-1). The perceived advantage of seignorage, or the power to borrow unlimited amounts in your own currency, ultimately becomes the curse that destroys the monetary hegemon. Eventually this must lead to a new order, the fifth in the last century and a half. This latest shift has been proceeding in a benign manner, as the role of the reserve currency seems to be evolving to a shared one, but the uncertainty surrounding the euro could threaten this gradual shift toward duality.

When the euro was being established during the 1990s, many economists warned the political leaders and other elites within the European Union that the project to establish a single currency could not work unless the economic and social structures underlying the new currency were far more unified than the political situation would allow. Convergence did not

Figure 4-1 Global Reserve Currencies

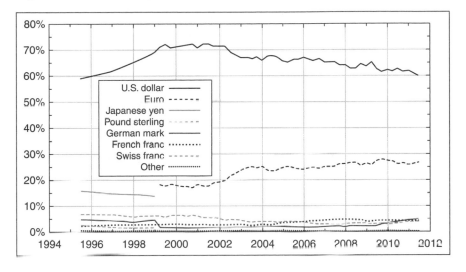

have to be absolute, but it needed to be reinforced by the social, economic, and legal systems supporting the still politically independent members of the new eurozone. That advice was ignored. The project went ahead, with only the commitment of the political leadership as its cohesive glue, plus the naïve hopes of the as-always economically unsophisticated populace.

It was, and still is, argued that the political will of the countries involved is so strong that all problems will be overcome. This smacks of hubris, as political power depends, at a minimum, on the acquiescence of the populace, if not its support; and without widespread economic well-being, this is not likely to be forthcoming, especially as the years of penury drag on. As politics is the art of the possible, political analysts cannot ignore that what is possible in any country derives from the social and economic realities of the society involved. What politicians can do and expect from their populace in Germany is far from what is politically possible in Greece or Italy.

A quick reading of *The Moral Basis of a Backward Society*, written in 1958 by Edward Banfield, with a major assist from his southern Italian wife, Laura, analyzing the impact of culture and social structure on economic and political development, should send chills down the spine of anyone hoping for a successful euro. Banfield notes that the comfortable assumption is often made that if the structure and incentives in the system are good, then the capital and the organizing skill will spring up and grow, allowing the society to advance. "This assumption overlooks the crucial importance of culture, [as] people live and think in different ways and some of these ways are radically inconsistent with the requirements of formal organization" (p. 8).

The Hobbesian reality of much of life in southern and Eastern Europe, which has been well known and documented by modern sociologists, should have been enough to convince any northern European political leader of the folly of expanding the eurozone to countries lacking a modern political society. Greece, Portugal, Cyprus, and Malta come immediately to mind as countries in which significant parts, if not the majority, of the society largely fit Banfield's definition of amoral familism, "unable to act together for the common good or indeed any end transcending the immediate material interest of the nuclear family" (p. 9).

Morality and public spiritedness are critical if taxes are to be paid and corruption is to be minimized, and when these qualities are lacking, no matter how draconian the externally imposed northern European regulations might be, they will be avoided and ignored in every instance. Countries with these cultural deficiencies will not succeed as part of the eurozone unless Brussels and the more civic-minded countries continue to pump money into them, just as Rome has pumped billions of euros into southern Italy through La Cassa per il Mezzogiorno for the past 50 years, with almost no results. (La Cassa per il Mezzogiorno was the Italian government's effort to build up southern Italy's economy but was thwarted by poor oversight and misguided investment.) Spain and Italy would seem to hug the borderline, with sections of the countries being more socially advanced and tending to enlightened self-interest or even public-spiritedness. We can hope that they are on the northern side of the divide, as the euro cannot survive without these two countries. It really doesn't matter how powerful the political will of the European leaders might be; what matters are the people. For generals to lead, their armies must follow them—not act for their own selfish, amoral interests.

The cultural and sociological issues are not the only ones that make the survival of the euro a long shot. Hard-nosed economic reality does too. The Nobel Prize juries are not always right, but they are a pretty good judge, and they actually voted against the euro way back in 1969 when they gave the first Nobel Prize in Economics to Jan Tinbergen of the Netherlands. In extremely simplified laymen's language, Tinbergen theorized and proved—in a social scientific way—that the financial managers of any government must have an equal or greater number of policy variables to adjust in order to manage the three economic outcomes that are important to a country's financial and economic success: employment, inflation, and current account balance.

Countries normally have four policy tools that they can manipulate as they manage the economy: the money supply, interest rates, fiscal balance, and currency level (or value). According to Tinbergen, four independent variables, correctly managed, should lead to continuing successful economic outcomes, and even three independent variables would be just enough. Unfortunately, the Maastricht Treaty, forged in the country of Tinbergen's birth, allows the eurozone countries only one independent variable (the fiscal balance), not four, and even fiscal maneuverability was constrained. Money supply, interest rates, and currency value are all established centrally, one-size-fits-all, under the control of the European Central Bank.

To keep their economies on track, national governments were almost immediately forced to break the Maastricht constraints—Germany was one of the first! Is it any wonder that in the past 12 years, European fiscal balances have been all over the place? Playing with the fiscal stance by changing the effective tax take and moving government spending has been the only way in which the financial authorities can manage their economies, but in the future, by following Merkel's tighter fiscal band, the individual governments will be almost powerless to manage them. Odds are that the situation will deteriorate further, not improve. While the total eurozone economy will theoretically be manageable, following Tinbergen's reasoning, as the whole is the one size that all must fit, each individual country will move erratically away from the average or convergence. By logically applying Tinbergen once again, it can even be argued that, over time, this situation will drive countries further and further from convergence, and recent empirical data already exhibit that tendency.

As convergence is an imperative for a functioning currency union, failing to reach it will eventually doom the euro. The only way to solve this lack of convergence, most likely manifested by a growing division between the richer and poorer countries, in a picture very similar to the disparity among cultures, is the continual transfer of financial support from the wealthier countries to the needier ones within the eurozone.

Although almost all eurozone politicians seem to wish it were not so, history has shown this to be the answer. The United States is an example of a transfer system, but, of course, so is any stable country, like Germany, France, or Italy. The richer parts support the poorer parts—they don't lend them money, they give it to them, as the money is never paid back. All of this is done through the tax system and various nationwide transfer programs, and it is hardly ever the subject of debate. In the next few years, Europe must either develop similar structures or take a giant step backward, retreating to a loose association of individual countries, each with its own currency.

At the same time that Europe is struggling with this great leap forward, two long-developing but slow-moving problems are approaching a possibly cataclysmic conclusion at some point within the next 10 to 20 years. Europe's debt is overwhelming it, and the continent's population is declining. The social welfare system, originated more than a century ago by Otto von Bismarck as part of his grand plan to keep the Socialist/Communist threat at bay and eventually adopted throughout Europe, is slowly bankrupting the major economies. As population growth slowly grinds to a halt during the next 40 years, the cost of the now-generous social programs will become overwhelming in relation to the size of the economy and the number of workers within it.

Neither of these problems can be solved with the flick of a switch. Not only have these payments become the centerpiece of the social compact between the governments and the voters, but these rights and offsetting responsibilities underlie the class structure and the fabric of national identity. Any changes in this compact, one that has survived and expanded throughout the last century despite global wars, deflation, and inflation, will be traumatic to individuals and extremely disruptive to the social peace. Despite the negative impact, however, these changes must occur, as these programs as currently structured cannot be financed because the working-age population will continue to decline as a percentage of the total population.

In the last year or so, it has become increasingly clear that parts of the European economy either have reached or are approaching the Ponzi stage of the long-term debt cycle as described by Hyman Minsky in *The Financial Instability Hypothesis* (1992). Currently, in some parts of Europe, many interest payments on bank and government debt cannot be made out of available funds and need to be financed with further borrowings. According to Minsky's hypothesis, economies move from stability toward instability over time. In stable economies, all borrowings, both the original capital and interest payments on it, can be repaid out of cash flow, corporate earnings, or government tax receipts. As the Minsky cycle moves toward a higher level of instability, only the interest can be paid; the capital cannot be and needs to be rolled over. In the worst stage, not even the interest on the loans can be repaid out of cash flow; it has to be borrowed, adding to the size of the outstanding loan. At that point, the Ponzi stage of the cycle, the system is extremely unstable, and some external event will eventually intervene, causing a chain of defaults and a collapse of the whole system.

Although not all banks and governments in Europe have reached this last stage, enough have done so to put the eurozone at risk of a string of defaults. What compounds the current problems beyond Minsky's simple example are the recent efforts to shore up the eurozone by adding more debt and more guarantees by higher financial authorities within a system that has no central authority and minimal political legitimacy. Beginning in 2008, when individual banks ran into credit problems, they were forced to turn to their local central banks, which supplied liquidity, committing their credit to these weak banks. Although the situation improved slightly for a while, in the weaker countries, the local central banks soon needed support from the European Central Bank (ECB) to shore up their national credit, as their national risk overwhelmed their countries' perceived taxing authority. These countries were threatening to go the way of Iceland (a non-eurozone country) in 2008, when the world financial crisis sparked a banking and economic meltdown leading to an IMF emergency bailout, as their governments could not support their own banking systems. By late 2011, the ECB was forced to step in throughout the entire eurozone, offering cheap and secure three-year credit to all the banks, against collateral. That collateral was often the very loans that would be used to refinance the Ponzi-like interest payments that could not be funded any other way.

This daisy chain of credit not only has involved the national governments in supporting private debt, but has also roped in the supranational ECB, which is now stuffed full of sovereign debt totaling more than 30 percent of the eurozone GDP. Individual countries, especially Germany, are also on the hook. The risk is not only very large but also highly centralized. Any significant default now puts the whole structure at risk.

This perilous financial situation depends on economies that have a declining workforce, a declining tax base, and low growth expectations. The shrinkage in the working-age population will continue to decrease the tax base of the European governments and, if services are to be maintained, will result in an increase in the tax burden on individual payers. According to a recent study by the UN, Europe has just turned the corner, beginning an annual shrinkage of the working-age population; it is currently decreasing at a rate of roughly −0.3 percent per

Figure 4-2 Annual Growth of Working-Age Population in Western Europe

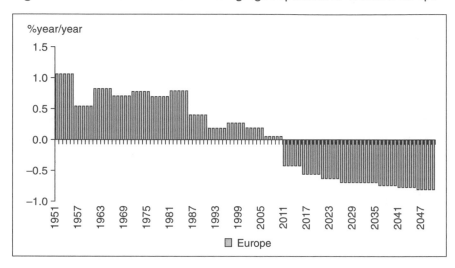

annum, which will expand to about −0.8 percent per annum by 2040, for a total decline of slightly less than 20 percent over the next 40 years. Consider that the working-age population has grown by roughly 35 percent over the last 50 years and the magnitude of the shock is obvious (see Figure 4-2).

With old age dependency ratios climbing from roughly 27 percent currently to about 43 percent over the same time span, the tax burden on the remaining workers will increase dramatically if the present retirement age and current level of benefits are to continue. Because of the longstanding social compact that makes any negative adjustment to the current privileges enjoyed by the citizens an anathema, either tax levels must rise or growth and labor productivity must increase dramatically. Although growth is the strategy that is being championed within the eurozone, the process of reducing administrative hurdles and restrictive labor practices is proving to be a challenge similar to that of reducing benefits. The widely praised efforts of Mario Monti, the recently installed technocrat prime minister of Italy, have attacked only the most trivial corners of red tape, but have generated a dramatic amount of pushback from taxi drivers, notaries, and pharmacists, among others.

Far more significant than these protected backwaters are the large government corporations that produce more than 50 percent of many basic economic goods within the eurozone. This statist industrial policy, harking back to Lenin's socialist New Economic Policy, when the government dominated the "commanding heights" of the Soviet economy, was adopted in varying degrees by the leading European states during the Depression and after World War II. Although there have been some privatizations and divestitures, railroads, airlines, electricity, oil production, steel, and many other heavy industries are still dominated or totally controlled by government companies.

The workers in these corporations are coddled and often hold the governments in their power, as Monti's trials in Italy illustrate. As a result, many of these state-owned organizations operate at a loss and are notoriously unproductive, but for Europe to survive intact, it is crucial that they become more efficient and profitable. A lurch higher in productivity or profitability would lessen the tax burden on the average citizen and greatly ameliorate the financial plight of the European governments. As Table 4-1 makes clear, the government payroll and purchases sometimes total more than 50 percent of the GDP. Among the EU countries, only Luxembourg has government expenditures under 40 percent. Among the OECD countries (Organisation for Economic Co-operation and Development), the Western Europeans have the highest level of government participation in the economy, a heavy burden to carry, as

Table 4-1 Tax Burden and Government Expenditures as a Percentage of GDP

Country	Tax Burden, % GDP	Government Expenditures, % GDP
Belgium	46.5	50.0
Denmark	49.0	51.8
Finland	43.2	49.5
France	44.6	52.8
Germany	40.6	43.7
Greece	35.1	46.8
Ireland	30.8	42.0
Italy	43.1	48.8
Luxembourg	36.5	37.2
Netherlands	39.8	45.9
Portugal	37.7	46.1
Russia	34.1	34.1
Spain	33.9	41.1
Switzerland	29.4	32.0
Turkey	23.5	23.4

statistics have shown a negative correlation between the size of government participation and GDP growth. The private sector is far more vibrant.

The odds do not favor a dramatic increase in growth while the Bismarckian social compact remains intact and the statist control of the commanding economic heights continues. The Wild West of Shenzhen and Silicon Valley is not about to erupt in the European heartland. Before that happens, the continent will have to undergo hellish hard times and an agonizing reassessment on a scale equal to, or greater than, that experienced by the Eastern Europeans after the collapse of Communism.

As the European population stalls and the birthrate continues to register far below the replacement level of 2.1, a growing awareness of the financial implications of this reality and the future that it implies will breed a deep psychological depression that will hold the continent back. The horrifying long-term impact of this shrinking process is that it will take many, many decades to reverse. European cities may still be beautiful and well preserved in 2100, but the countryside will be drained of people and less vibrant. House prices cannot move higher when there is a continual decline in family formations. As a result, residential construction and renovation will stagnate, and abandoned homes and towns will be seen everywhere.

Historical records, always better in Europe, note three previous times when the population declined: through the first half of the seventeenth century, in most of the fourteenth century, and through the tenth century and into the early eleventh century. Although each of these periods seems to have been dominated by specific social fears—expectations of the end of the world around 1000, multiple plagues in the fourteenth century, and wars in the seventeenth century—they all exhibit a shrinkage of land under cultivation, a decline in the arts, and a reduction in rational activity, combined with an increase in uncivilized activities like witch trials, homicides, and atrocities.

Although modern society can be expected to do better, there is a high probability that Europe will suffer a brain drain as the stagnation that is so apparent at home drives the best to other parts of the world. The most that Europe can expect is a worldwide appreciation for its long-term role as a font of civilization, a quiet place to retire or visit. Offsetting this dowagerlike existence will be an increasing in-migration of Africans and Middle Easterners taking advantage of the job opportunities that cannot be filled by native Europeans. Although the next generations won't be able to bring Europe out of its swoon, if the three previous instances of population decline prove at all instructive, Europe will arise stronger than ever in the twenty-second century, sparked by the new blood from outside its borders.

Taking a slightly shorter-term view of Europe and the euro, a more recent historical example might be appropriate. In 1815 (after the French Revolution of 1789 had upset the European monarchies, setting off a tumultuous 26 years capped by more than a decade of war in which Napoleon's armies upset the entire military, political, and judicial landscape of Europe), the triumphant old guard put Europe back together again. Count Metternich and the others put all the pieces back where they had been before, as best they could, and promised never to let this happen again.

The concept behind the activities creating the European Coal and Steel Community in 1950, leading up to the Treaty of Rome in 1956, bears more than a passing resemblance to that of the Congress of Vienna in 1815. The architects of the peace in Austria wanted things to return to a better time and were successful for the following 33 years, but then a series of government-shaking riots erupted in the major European capitals as the people began to react to the economic and social changes that had altered their relationship to their governments. In the next 23 years, between 1848 and 1871, the political landscape of Europe was redrawn in a long, but stop-and-go process in which Italy and Germany became countries, Switzerland and Austria were reconstructed, and France was finally firmly set on the republican road. After 1871, Europe was at peace until World War I. Jean Monnet and Walter Schumann were even more successful than Metternich, as their reconstruction of the pre–1914 idyll has proved more durable, lasting from 1950 through today. The six original members of the European Union put the pieces back together after the 31 years of carnage beginning with World War I and running through the rampages of Hitler and World War II, swearing never again.

These political architects have succeeded beyond their wildest dreams, but going back to the past works only for a while. The impact of scientific advances and the industrial and postindustrial revolutions means that it cannot work forever. Europe in 1848 was politically the same as it was in 1788, but economically, scientifically, and socially, it was not. It needed to be changed, and the result was 23 years of intermittent revolution. Europe today has a political structure that is very similar to that of 1913, but economically, scientifically, and socially, it is incredibly different.

Change is necessary. How many years of political and economic crises will it take before Europe finds an appropriate new form that matches the realities of today? If we were to be optimistic, the answer would be several decades, but with the population decline and the Minsky debt crisis added to the list of systemic problems, it could take much longer to find a solution.

Valuing the euro through the coming years of traumatic changes in the eurozone, within the wider frames of Europe and the world, is not really possible, but some major tendencies are obvious. Although the euro is the second most important currency in the world today, whether one considers trading volumes or its position as an investment vehicle in terms of reserves, fixed-income markets, or equities, it will decline in importance over the next decades. Although it is unlikely to disappear, the process of restructuring will force a negative reassessment. This process, compounded by the debt crisis and the political struggles within some of the eurozone countries, will force Europe to retreat within itself and will see the rest of the world standing apart from its problems.

Without dramatic action, the continent will seem like the modern-day version of the Austro-Hungarian Empire, tottering toward its eventual demise. By mid-century, its population will drop to less than 4 percent of the global total, and its GDP will probably be in the high teens, a far drop from today's prominence. The world will grow, but Europe will not. It will be dwarfed by China and India, the emerging Asian giants, while Korea, Indonesia, and Thailand will each surpass the GDPs of the largest European countries. Brazil will outpace Europe as well. Although the United States will retain its dominant position, because of its economic weakness, it will be forced to share its preeminence with the Asians.

As the reserve currency structure is not likely to survive in its current form, the dollar will probably share the responsibility for global liquidity with a basket of other currencies and commodities, but the euro is unlikely to play a major role, having been replaced by the Asians and others. Because Europe will not be central to world development, it will slide into a position similar to that of the United Kingdom today. The euro will be forced to adapt to the economic policies of the more dominant countries. As sterling moves primarily in relation to the euro, and Australia trades as a satellite of the Chinese economy, so too, will the euro react to the Asian and North American lead.

CHAPTER 5

THE FUTURE OF THE EUROZONE: AN AMICABLE DIVORCE IS BETTER THAN AN UNHAPPY MARRIAGE

MEGAN GREENE

"The one currency is irreversible."
—Mario Draghi, December 2011

A number of myths surround the euro crisis, the most common of which is that the best outcome for all involved would be for the eurozone (the countries that use the euro common currency and the European Central Bank) to stay together in its current formation. It is difficult for analysts and policy makers to contemplate the practicalities of the eurozone's actually breaking up. After all, the common currency was never a purely financial arrangement—it was part of the broader political project to prevent a return to war in Europe as well.

Even partially dismantling the eurozone would be a logistical nightmare, with contracts needing to be redenominated into new currencies and with cascading defaults potentially being triggered across the region. This would undoubtedly be painful and messy. But so is the endless path of retrenchment and bailouts on which the debtor and creditor countries in the eurozone have embarked.

What's more, history is not on the eurozone's side; the vast majority of currency unions have eventually been torn apart. Only those in the United States of America and the United Kingdom have survived. The European Commission, the European Central Bank (ECB), and the International Monetary Fund (IMF)—together referred to as the "troika"—have gone to great lengths to keep all 17 member states in the eurozone. But it seems increasingly likely that some of the weaker countries will eventually peel out of the euro area, starting with Greece. This should not alarm us. Both the countries that leave the eurozone and those that remain as members of the common currency will be better off for this parting of the ways. In the medium to long term, an amicable, albeit expensive, divorce is preferable to an unhappy marriage.

The Benefits to Greece of Exiting

Greece has a long history as a trailblazer, whether as the cradle of democracy or for its numerous mathematical, scientific, philosophical, and athletic developments over the centuries. In the next few years, however, Greece will blaze a trail of a very different sort by becoming the first country to choose to default and exit the euro. It will not be the last country to do so. European leaders have gone out of their way to declare Greece a unique case, but Greece will come to be a model for how the weaker countries will be handled.

After months of negotiations, in March 2012, the troika and the Greek government finally agreed to a deal on a second support package for Greece and on private-sector involvement (PSI) to reduce Greece's stock of debt. But this deal will fail to return Greece to fiscal sustainability, particularly given that the second support package agreed upon involves further austerity measures and structural reforms, both of which will undermine economic growth in the short term. This, in turn, will send Greece's debt-to-GDP ratio soaring higher as output contracts.

The planned structural reforms are aimed at opening up product and labor markets so that Greece can regain its competitiveness and eventually return to sustainable growth. But prior to the second support program, the Greek government was effective only at legislating structural reforms rather than actually implementing them. There is no reason to expect any turnaround on this, particularly given rising levels of opposition to reform among Greece's public, politicians, and trade unions. The second bailout and PSI deal will temporarily address Greece's stock-of-debt issue, but it will do nothing to address the much more important flow-of-debt issue. If the Greek government fails to liberalize its economy and boost competitiveness over the next few years, Greece's debt burden will ramp right back up over time.

While the Greek government is often accused of having done nothing to comply with the terms of its bailout agreements, this is not strictly true. Woefully few structural reforms have been implemented, but the fiscal adjustment in Greece over the past few years has been significant, with public- and private-sector wages and pensions having been cut sharply.

The middle class has been hit hard by austerity. But while there have been some violent antiausterity protests in Syntagma Square in central Athens, the vast majority of Greeks believe that they are better off in the euro than outside it.

It also seems unlikely that the troika will abandon Greece in the short term. During negotiations on the second support program, it was clear that patience with Greece had waned amongst the eurozone's creditor countries. Senior German and Dutch policy makers were openly discussing a Greek exit from the eurozone, something that would have been unfathomable just a year before. Despite this, however, there are two reasons for the troika to continue to keep Greece on life support. First, before the troika turns off the funding taps for Greece, it aims to create a firewall between the rest of the eurozone and a Greek default and exit from the eurozone. Second, the German elections scheduled for September 2013 made it unlikely that Chancellor Merkel would allow her election campaign to be clouded by whatever would be unleashed by a Greek default and exit.

However, with Germany's elections over in late 2013 and the Greeks further squeezed by new austerity measures, both Greece and the troika will consider alternatives to the current cycle of austerity and bailouts. Greece will face a stark choice about how to return to growth. On the one hand, it can continue along its current path of austerity as a means of achieving an internal devaluation, thereby regaining competitiveness and eventually seeing its economic performance improve. But this would probably result in a decade of depression. On the other hand, Greece could choose to exit the eurozone, reissue the drachma, and allow the currency to devalue significantly. This would see Greece regaining competitiveness and returning to growth much more quickly. Exiting the eurozone inevitably entails sovereign and bank defaults and bank runs.

This scenario is painful, but increasingly, it has seemed that Greece would experience these things anyhow, whether sticking with the common currency or not. The country might as well benefit from a nominal devaluation to provide an immediate boost to economic growth.

A Greek exit involves the troika and Greece coming together and agreeing that an amicable divorce is needed because the relationship is simply not working any longer. The troika then provides Greece with bridge financing. This cushions the financial blow of exiting the eurozone, but with continuing conditionality attached, it could also serve as a stick to ensure that Greece finally implements the structural reforms necessary for the country to achieve sustainable growth.

Opening Pandora's Box: Who Will Choose to Follow Greece?

A Greek default and exit from the eurozone will be painful and messy. Nevertheless, some of the other weaker eurozone countries will still choose to follow in Greece's footsteps in order to return to growth more quickly.

Unlike Greece, Portugal has so far managed to achieve the fiscal targets set out for it in the troika's bailout program. However, Portugal's success has been largely due to a series of one-off measures—such as shifting banks' pension funds to the government's social security budget—that cannot be repeated in the future. This, combined with the fact that Portugal's GDP will be contracting significantly over the next few years, suggests that Portugal will not continue to meet its fiscal targets. According to the first Portuguese bailout program, the country is expected to return to the markets in 2013. This is highly unlikely, given how unsustainably high Portugal's borrowing costs have risen during the crisis, and the country is likely to follow Greece's model in requesting not only a second bailout package from the troika, but also a reduction of its debt burden in a PSI deal.

As in Greece, PSI in Portugal will address the stock-of-debt problem but will not deal with the flow-of-debt issue over time. In order to regain competitiveness and return to sustainable growth, therefore, Portugal will face the same choice that Greece currently faces: either Portugal can experience a decade of depression, or it can choose to exit from the eurozone and undergo a nominal devaluation.

Ireland might have a fighting chance at returning to growth within the eurozone, but this is looking increasingly uncertain. Ireland's GDP will stagnate at best in the short to medium term as its main export markets—the United States, the United Kingdom, and the eurozone—go into stall speed or recession. Ireland is entirely reliant on exports for growth, with domestic demand exerting a negative drag on GDP.

Furthermore, concerns about Ireland's banking sector remain. While the number of mortgages in arrears has risen sharply, mortgage defaults have yet to crystallize. The longer mortgage defaults are delayed, the larger they tend to be. Reforms in the personal insolvency regime in Ireland will allow individuals to write off some of their debts, including mortgages. This should reduce the cost of mortgage default for the banks, but they may still need to be recapitalized. Of the €35 billion earmarked for the banking sector in the original bailout package, only around €16.5 billion was used, with the remainder being reallocated to the Irish government in order to delay the sovereign's having to return to the bond markets. If Irish banks need to be recapitalized, the funding will once again have to come from the government, pushing the Irish sovereign debt burden up even higher.

But even if Ireland can make its creditors whole, there is a significant risk that it will choose not to. Once Greece and Portugal have defaulted and exited from the eurozone, Ireland may decide on a strategic default and eurozone exit. Unlike Portugal and Greece, Ireland already benefits from open product and labor markets and a highly skilled labor force. Rather than continuing to implement austerity measures, Ireland may choose to default, reissue its national currency, the punt, and use a nominal devaluation to return to growth quickly.

Buying Time for Italy and Spain

The response to the eurozone crisis has centered on buying time for the single currency's weaker, peripheral members. Particular attention has been focused on Italy and Spain, because the sheer size of both their economies and their debt burdens threatens to transmit the crisis to the currency's core countries. The aim has been to buy enough time for Italy and Spain to implement structural reforms and for those reforms to have taken hold and begun to facilitate growth. This is a lengthy process that generally takes about five to ten years, particularly in countries like these two, with rigid labor markets and no control over monetary policy.

The troika has relied on two measures to buy time for Italy and Spain. The first is the ECB's three-year, long-term refinancing operation (LTRO). The LTRO immediately relieved pressure on Italy and Spain in the sovereign bond markets, with banks using the ECB's cheap financing in part to buy domestic sovereign debt. This was particularly the case in Italy, where banks were so exposed to Italian sovereign debt that they chose to double down on it, taking advantage of the cheap loans and using the LTRO to pick up more Italian debt, in the hope of reducing the chances of Italy's undergoing a debt restructuring.

Given that the euro crisis is, at its very core, a balance of payments and growth crisis, the ECB's three-year LTRO is a game changer only if it can help rebalance the eurozone economies through an adjustment in real effective exchange rates, or if it can significantly improve the periphery's growth prospects. The LTRO will help to smooth out the deleveraging process that eurozone banks are undergoing. This means that the severity of the credit crunch that might have occurred without the LTRO will be mitigated. However, banks are unlikely to use liquidity from the LTRO operations to lend, and consequently the degree to which the LTRO will support growth is limited.

The LTRO succeeded in suppressing sovereign bond yields for Italy and Spain in the immediate term. If investors once again shun Italian and Spanish sovereign debt, the ECB is likely to offer additional LTROs or other extraordinary operations. However, there are limitations to how many LTROs can be offered and how much take-up there can be. Some members of the ECB's governing council have expressed opposition to further LTROs, and ultimately ECB president Mario Draghi is likely to come into conflict with the German central bank, the Bundesbank, which is extremely wary of these types of operations that cause the ECB's balance sheet to balloon.

Furthermore, banks must provide collateral in exchange for liquidity from the LTROs. While the collateral requirements have been significantly widened, banks will eventually run out of qualifying collateral. And while the LTRO differs in many ways from the sort of quantitative easing (QE) programs that the United States and the United Kingdom have embarked on, there are some parallels. Specifically, limited liquidity does not solve solvency issues (although unlimited liquidity can), and with each round of LTROs, we expect the relief in pressure on peripheral bond yields to be milder.

Ultimately, the relief in the peripheral sovereign bond markets resulting from the LTROs will be undermined by real, hard economic data. The Italian and Spanish governments are implementing austerity measures and have announced ambitious structural reform programs. In the short term, both austerity and structural reforms undermine growth. Consequently, economic activity in Italy and Spain will slow sharply over at least the next year. This will cause the pressure on Italian and Spanish bond markets to return, with borrowing costs for both countries eventually becoming unsustainable.

The second measure the troika has relied on to buy time for Italy and Spain is a firewall to take the two countries out of the bond markets once the LTRO euphoria wears off and borrowing costs rise again. At the time of writing, the firewall is to be cobbled together between the EU bailout funds—the European Financial Stability Facility (EFSF) and the European Stability Mechanism (ESM)—and bilateral loans to the IMF. For the firewall to work, both its EU and its IMF elements must be large enough. This is far from guaranteed, and failure on this point could trigger a massive escalation of the crisis.

On the EU side of the firewall, there are currently two funds in place: the EFSF, which has around €250 billion in available funding, and the €500 billion ESM. The former is due to replace the ESM, but the only way to amass enough funds to cover Italy and Spain's financing needs for a few years is to run the EFSF and the ESM concurrently. There has been some German reluctance to allow the two EU bailout funds to be additive, although Chancellor Merkel has indicated that Germany might allow this. On the IMF side, many countries have indicated their reluctance to contribute to a firewall until the eurozone devotes more of its own collective resources to solving its crisis.

If the three-year LTROs buy a year for Italy and Spain by suppressing their sovereign bond yields for that long, and if both countries were then to request official financing, the eurozone's total firewall would be sufficient to take all the weaker eurozone countries out of the markets until mid-2015 at the latest. However, some official financing will need to be held back in case another eurozone country—such as Belgium—is in need of a bailout. Furthermore, some of the firewall would have to be earmarked to recapitalize Italian and Spanish banks should those two countries have to restructure their debt, as has been done in Greece (€50 billion of Greece's second support package is earmarked to recapitalize its banks following PSI). Thus, not all of the firewall would be allocated to Italy and Spain, and we expect that both countries would have to return to the markets in late 2014 or early 2015.

It is unlikely that either government will have both succeeded in implementing deeply unpopular structural reforms and seen those reforms begin to support growth by late 2014. In Italy, an election in April 2013 is likely to produce greater political instability, which in turn could threaten to derail or significantly slow the implementation of structural reforms. In Spain, the property market has yet to find its bottom, and mortgage defaults will require the state to step in with further aid for the banks, requiring ever more austerity to try to regain control of the public finances. If Italy and Spain face unsustainable borrowing costs when the firewall runs out, they will need to avail themselves of either another bailout (from outside public funds) or a bail-in (recapitalizing from within). It is difficult to imagine where more funding could be found for a bailout, given that the firewall will have already included IMF money, and consequently Italy and Spain will probably be forced to undergo an orderly debt restructuring.

Like that of Greece, a debt restructuring in Italy and Spain would address the countries' stock-of-debt issue, making them appear more fiscally sustainable and therefore giving them more time to try to address their flow-of-debt problem. This would require implementing structural reforms to open product and labor markets, unwind imbalances, and engineer an internal devaluation. If Italy and Spain manage to restructure their economies as well as their debt over the next five to ten years, they have a fighting chance of finding a path toward sustainable growth within the eurozone. But there is a high risk that their plans for structural reform will be sidelined or decelerated by social unrest, opposition from vested interests, or cyclical economic shocks. If this is the case, then Italy and Spain will face the same choice about returning to growth as Greece: either they could continue along the same path of austerity and retrenchment for a decade of depression, or they could choose to exit from the eurozone and return to growth much more quickly.

Why the Core Would Benefit from a Eurozone Breakup

Each of the eurozone's weaker countries is likely to face a choice between prolonged retrenchment inside the single currency and an accelerated return to growth outside it. While this will be painful and messy, it is the lesser of two evils, not only for the weaker countries, but for the core countries in the eurozone as well.

The core countries have two main courses of action they could pursue instead of supporting the weaker countries while they restructure their debt and exit from the eurozone in a managed fashion. The first option would be to pull the plug on the weaker countries, cutting off their funding and letting them fend for themselves. This would be a disaster for all parties, causing the crisis to spread like wildfire to the core. It is clearly not on the table. The second alternative would be for the core countries to keep the peripheral countries on life support indefinitely, effectively turning the core-periphery relationship into an endless unhappy marriage.

To maintain such an unhappy marriage, the euro's core countries would need to agree either to unlimited fiscal subsidies for the weaker countries through joint and several liabilities (such as eurobonds) or to fiscal transfers. But eurobonds can emerge only after political union and a pooling of assets within the eurozone have been achieved. This is a long-term process, and there is very little chance that eurozone leaders could achieve this in the time frame necessary to keep the weaker countries in the common currency area. More likely, the eurozone's unhappy marriage of core and periphery would involve creating a fiscal transfer union, or debt sharing, in which strong countries or states end up subsidizing weaker countries or states, as in the United States. This is an extremely risky and expensive venture, however.

Weaker countries would lack incentives to undergo the difficult and painful task of rebalancing their economies if they knew that they could turn to the wealthier eurozone countries for handouts instead. Transfers to the weaker countries are already vehemently opposed by the stronger, wealthier countries of the core. Furthermore, if the core countries were to provide all of the weaker eurozone countries with unlimited fiscal transfers, the core countries' own balance sheets would become impaired, and they would end up requiring bailouts themselves.

While the introduction of eurobonds is too long-term a project to be completed in time to prevent the exit of some weaker countries from the eurozone, such exits from the periphery would make it easier for the remaining core countries to create joint and several liabilities in a common eurobond.

The euro's core countries do not trust the fiscal responsibility of their peripheral counterparts. This was highlighted by the agreement of the fiscal compact, an initiative spearheaded by Germany to impose limits on the fiscal imbalances that euro zone member states are allowed to accrue. Eurozone leaders touted the fiscal compact as an early step toward fiscal union, but at the time of its agreement, it represented nothing of the sort. It was an attempt to get the weaker euro countries to mimic Germany's fiscal dynamic, thereby placing the entire onus for adjustment on the periphery and ensuring that drastic fiscal adjustment would drive the eurozone's weaker countries deeper into recession.

Given Germany's obsessive insistence on fiscal responsibility as a pillar of the eurozone, the exit of weaker countries from the common currency area could provide the impetus for the stronger countries to move toward creating a true fiscal union. Currently, the core countries are unwilling to pool their liabilities with those of the weaker countries because of concerns that they will be subsidizing those countries forever and will therefore see their borrowing costs rise. But if the eurozone loses its weaker members, the smaller eurozone that would result would consist of countries with a greater reputation for fiscal responsibility. Such a change in the profile of the membership might lead the strongest, wealthiest countries to become less opposed to issuing eurobonds.

Smaller but Stronger

Eurozone leaders have said over and over again that they will do whatever it takes to protect the common currency. Most people have interpreted this to mean that eurozone leaders are committed to keeping all 17 current member states in the eurozone. But doing what is needed for the euro to survive is not necessarily the same as doing what is needed to keep all of its current members on board. Nor is continued participation in the single currency necessarily the best economic strategy for all of its current members.

Ultimately, the best solution for both the weaker and the stronger eurozone members may be to allow at least some of the former to abandon the common currency in an amicable divorce. Trying to muddle through together may make matters worse rather than better for all concerned. Even if eurozone leaders manage to buy enough time so that the common currency survives the current crisis intact, regular boom-and-bust business cycles indicate that there will be another fiscal or financial shock in the eurozone over the next decade. Without a fundamental unwinding of imbalances in the eurozone and the creation of an optimal currency union with fiscal transfers or pooled liabilities, the next fiscal shock is likely to see the eurozone back in crisis. Similarly, decisive action is required to restore economic growth within the weak peripheral countries.

The exit of the weaker states from the common currency area would achieve both of these aims, giving the periphery the flexibility to return to growth quickly, while allowing the core to accelerate moves toward the kind of fiscal union that is needed to underpin the long-term viability of the common currency. This kind of partial breakup of the single currency would be traumatic and complicated. But it would not mark the demise of the euro. On the contrary, it would put it on a stronger footing. That which does not kill us makes us stronger.

CHAPTER 6

REBALANCING GROWTH IN CHINA: THE ROLE OF THE YUAN IN THE POLICY PACKAGE

Anoop Singh and Papa N'Diaye[1]

"We need to quicken the pace of internationalization of our capital markets to improve the global status of the yuan."
—Yi Gang, Deputy Governor, People's
Bank of China, March 2011

The Chinese economy has achieved a remarkable transformation over a span of three decades to become the world's second largest economy. More than 380 million jobs have been created, and about 500 million people have been lifted out of poverty. This great achievement reflects years of reforms to open up the Chinese economy and make it more market-oriented, particularly to encourage the production of tradable goods. This has allowed China to better exploit its comparative advantages and benefit from the economies of scale afforded by global markets.

However, the economy's size and large presence in world markets today mean that this outward growth strategy is approaching high levels by historical standards and could run into natural limits. In addition, China's heavy orientation toward the production and export of tradable goods has come at the cost of a smaller nontradable sector, particularly services, and low private consumption, as households' savings have been mobilized through the banking system and transferred to corporations through low-interest-rate loans.

Continuing the current growth model translates into maintaining the transfer of resources from households to corporations and preserving a playing field that is highly favorable to the tradable sector—a task that has become increasingly challenging since the global financial crisis broke out. Indeed, the global financial crisis has put an end to the credit-fueled consumption boom that started in the United States and other advanced economies in the early 2000s. Lasting damage to households' and financial institutions' balance sheets, the need for sizable fiscal consolidation in the future, and likely steps toward more stringent financial regulation all forecast that domestic demand in these economies is unlikely to return to precrisis growth rates. Weaker growth in the advanced economies would mean that an important source of demand for China's exports remains subdued.

The imperative to change China's growth model is well recognized by the Chinese government. Since the onset of the global financial crisis, the government has made commendable progress in expanding social safety nets and allocating greater resources to pension, healthcare, and education systems. This should help boost private consumption by lowering precautionary savings, but more needs to be done to promote a sustained rebalancing of the Chinese economy.

In particular, the authorities recognize that exchange-rate appreciation is a key ingredient in the transformation of China's economic growth model. The undervaluation of the currency has been holding back progress in other areas that would further promote economic rebalancing. For example, an undervalued currency creates distortions in relative prices that typically act as headwinds to the government's efforts to raise household income and to develop the service sector. In addition, it reduces the capability of running a more proactive and independent monetary policy with higher real interest rates. Higher domestic interest rates would better price capital and allow its more efficient allocation, while promoting financial intermediation in a more inclusive way by providing greater returns to small depositors. At the same time, the significant and sustained need to absorb liquidity from large-scale foreign currency intervention that China has experienced constrains the government's ability to move ahead with financial liberalization. Liberalizing the financial sector in an environment with excess raises the risks of bubbles and other imbalances in asset and goods markets that could translate into greater macroeconomic volatility.

This chapter reviews the main imbalances of the Chinese economy, the reforms needed to address them, the role of the yuan, and the benefits of rebalancing growth.

What Are the Imbalances in the Chinese Economy?

China's dependence on external demand is larger than the OECD (Organisation for Economic Co-operation and Development) average, investment is above most benchmarks

based on international comparisons and model-based estimates, and private consumption is at one of the lowest levels
in the world and is too low given China's level of development. These factors are reflected in China's large current
account surplus.

China Has a Large Dependence on External Demand

China's growth relies heavily on external demand, and this
dependence has increased in recent years. During 2001–2009, net
exports and investment by private and public entities in areas
predominantly linked to building greater capacity in tradable
sectors accounted for more than 60 percent of China's growth,
up from 40 percent in the 1990s (see Figure 6-1). This is much
larger than the 2001–2008 average for the G-7 (16 percent), the
euro area (30 percent), and the rest of Asia (35 percent).

Figure 6-1 Contribution to Growth

(Percent of Total GDP Growth)

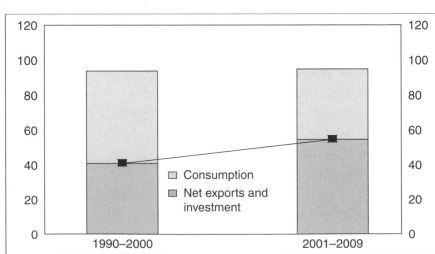

However, gross trade flows may overstate China's external dependence, since they don't take into account the growing significance of cross-border supply chain networks through vertical integration. This refers to an organizational production structure that extends over several stages of manufacturing, transforming raw materials and other inputs into final goods. Its significance is that actually, a smaller share of domestic value added is included in exports than is suggested by the gross trade figures. Indeed, China imports significant amounts of raw material, intermediate goods, and capital goods from commodity producers and the rest of Asia that go into the production of final consumption and capital goods, which are mainly destined for mature markets, such as the United States, the euro area, and Japan. And, in that process, China adds a limited, albeit increasing, share of value added. But even so, alternative measures of exposure based on the share of value added linked to external demand show China's high dependence on external demand. The latest International Monetary Fund (IMF) staff estimates of the contribution of external demand to China's value added range between 25 percent and 40 percent when the investment related to exports is taken into account (see Figure 6-2).²

This large contribution of China's exports to the country's overall growth reflects a rapid growth in exports (on average by 18.5 percent since the end of the 1990s), and also an increase in the domestic content of these exports. This, in turn, has led to a substantial expansion of China's global market share. China's share of exports in global markets has nearly quadrupled over the past 15 years, rising from around 3 percent in 1995 to about 12 percent in 2009 (see Figure 6-3), and it has doubled since China's entry into the World Trade Organization

Figure 6-2 Selected Asia: Share of Export Value Added in GDP

(Percent of GDP)

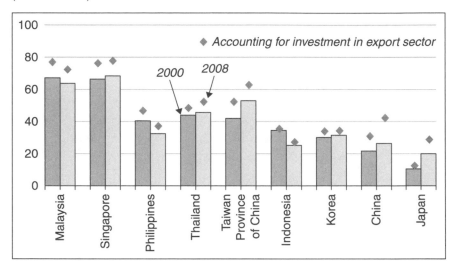

Sources: Japan External Trade Organization (JETRO), Asian Input Output Table (2000), OECD, UN Comtrade, and CEIC Data.

(WTO) at the end of 2001. Maintaining such a trajectory would require lower prices in a range of industries, which could be achieved through a combination of increases in productivity, lower profits, and higher implicit or explicit subsidies to industry. While unprecedented gains in market share may yet occur, the evidence from key Chinese industries such as steel, shipbuilding, and machine tools suggests that it will be difficult to accommodate price cuts within existing profit margins and productivity gains. For example, Guo and N'Diaye (2009) show that while profit margins in these industries range between 5 and 10 percent, the price cuts that would be required to maintain market share gains would be on the order of 15 to 45 percent.

Figure 6-3   Market Share of Selected Economies Since Growth Takeoff

(Percent)

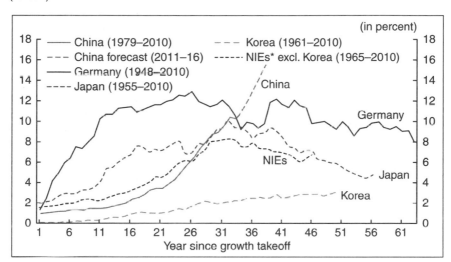

* NIEs are newly industrialized economies

Investment Is One of the Highest in the World

Investment in China as a share of GDP has reached about 50 percent of GDP, up from slightly less than 30 percent in 1982. This level of investment is high by most standards, including when compared with other countries with a similar development strategy and countries with similar income levels (see Figure 6-4). Investment is financed primarily through retained earnings and bank loans. Most of the investment has been concentrated in the manufacturing sector, encouraged by various cost advantages, including a low cost of capital and utilities, pollution, energy, and land; tax incentives; and an undervalued currency, as well as a large pool of savings.

Figure 6-4 Investment-GDP Ratio

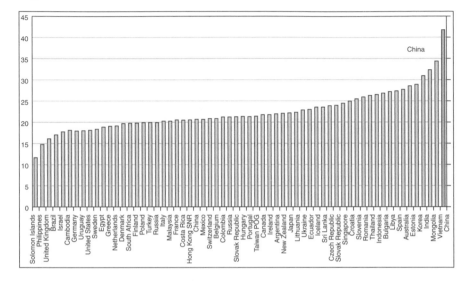

- *Land and water.* In China, all land belongs to the state, and local governments have the discretion to sell industrial land use rights to companies for up to 50 years. In many cases, industrial land is provided for free to enterprises to attract investment. For water, the price in China is about one-third of the average of a sample of international comparators.
- *Energy.* Cross-country data on the cost of energy show that the price of gasoline in China is relatively low, although it is similar to that in the United States. For electricity, the cost is also somewhat below the average of international comparisons, although discussions with private counterparts reveal that many companies are able to negotiate significant discounts to the regulated price. Having said this, China is making progress in bringing energy costs in line with international levels: oil product

Figure 6-5 Price of Energy in China Compared to That in Other Nations

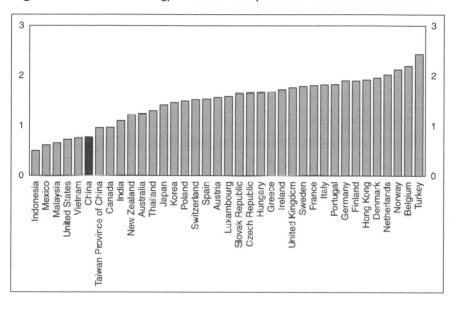

prices have been indexed to a weighted basket of international crude prices, natural gas prices were increased by 25 percent in May 2010, and preferential power tariffs for energy-intensive industries have been revoked (see Figure 6-5).

- *Capital.* By various cross-country measures, the cost of capital in China appears low. Using data on 37,000 firms across 53 countries, IMF staff estimates show that the real cost of capital—defined as a weighted average of the real cost of bank loans, bonds, and equity—faced by Chinese listed firms is below the global average (see Figure 6-6).[3] Capital looks especially cheap when compared to its high productivity in China. In particular, country-specific estimates of the marginal product of reproducible capital (i.e., capital adjusted for land) show that the real rate of

Figure 6-6 Real Cost of Capital

(2005–2009)

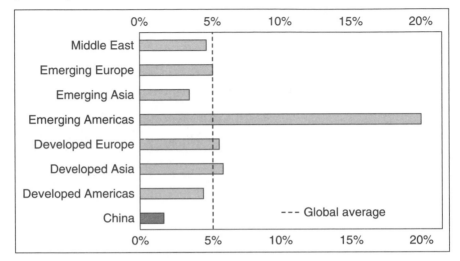

return on investment in China is much higher than real loan rates, with the discrepancy being larger than in many economies.

How long can China sustain such a high rate of investment? Persistent high rates of investment run the risk of creating over-capacity in many sectors because domestic or external consumption might not rise fast enough to absorb the new output. This will exert deflationary pressure; increase nonperforming loans in the banking system, as companies will be less profitable than anticipated at the time the projects were being financed; and ultimately lead to deterioration in the general government's fiscal position. Such a buildup of excess capacity would also have consequences for the rest of the world, as excess capacity in the manufacturing sector in China would further dampen tradable prices in global markets, potentially creating trade tensions.

Corporate Savings in China Are High

There are numerous reasons for China's high corporate savings. First, the low cost of capital gives Chinese firms a competitive edge and creates incentives for capital- and energy-intensive means of production (see Figure 6-7) Studies estimate that the total value of China's factor market distortions (labor, land, energy, capital, and so on) could be almost 10 percent of GDP.[4] Second, there is a lack of market contestability (i.e., competition), with many firms enjoying oligopoly positions in domestic markets,[5] while at the same time smaller firms (which have limited access to financing) save to ensure that they can fund profitable projects. Finally, corporations are not subject to the same contestability of ownership that is seen in other systems, which may lead these firms to have less incentive to distribute profits in the form of dividends.

Figure 6-7 Cost of Capital in China Relative to That in Other Countries

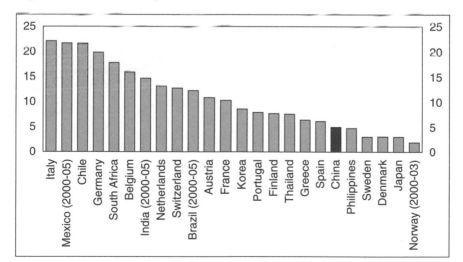

Household Consumption Is Much Lower than It Should Be

China's private consumption as a share of GDP has declined from around 55 percent in the early 1980s to around 37 percent in 2008 (see Figure 6-8). The decline in the country's share of private consumption during the early development stages is not in itself a surprise—savings naturally rise at early stages of development, as households move away from subsistence levels of income, and greater capital accumulation is needed to finance investment and growth. However, the size of the fall in China's private consumption share stands out. Reasons put forward to explain the downward trend in China's share of private consumption relate both to households' saving rate and income and to statistics.[6] Be that as it may, recent cross-country

Figure 6-8 Cumulative Change in Ratio of Private Consumption to GDP: Estimated Contribution of Household Disposable Income and Household Saving Rate

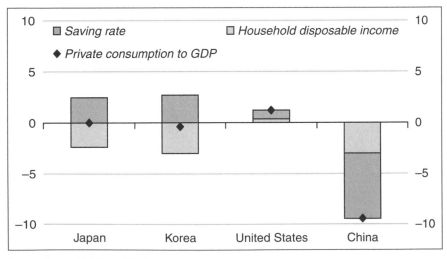

Source: Guo and N'Diaye (2009).

evidence suggests that the low consumption-to-GDP ratio in China has relatively little to do with country-specific behavioral factors. Instead, the evidence shows that it can largely be explained by the low, and declining, share of household disposable income and a rising saving rate. The high household saving rate in China in part reflects precautionary saving to offset the lack of social safety nets. Limited access to financial services, including consumer credit and housing finance, may also play a role.

On the Supply Side, China's Export-Oriented Growth Model Has Resulted in a Small Services Sector, and Growth Is Less Employment-Intensive than It Should Be

These households' large savings are limited both by the lack of investment opportunities at home and capital controls on investment abroad. This, together with a low cost of capital, the underpricing of other factor inputs, and an undervalued exchange rate, has provided Chinese firms with a competitive edge in global markets and created incentives for capital-intensive means of production. The share of the tradable sector in China's GDP is more than 10 percentage points above the world average for low- and middle-income countries, and as a corollary, the share of services in GDP is generally lower (see Figure 6-9). With the services sector typically being more labor-intensive, China's export-oriented growth has naturally translated into a relatively low employment growth compared to other economies' experience and China's fundamentals. China's average annual GDP growth of 11 percent over the past 7 years has been associated with only about 1 percent increase in employment (see Figure 6-10).

Figure 6-9   Excess Share of Industry in GDP

(In Percentage Points; Country Industry Share Minus Industry Share of Peer Group)

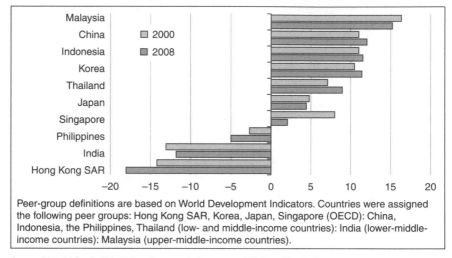

Peer-group definitions are based on World Development Indicators. Countries were assigned the following peer groups: Hong Kong SAR, Korea, Japan, Singapore (OECD): China, Indonesia, the Philippines, Thailand (low- and middle-income countries): India (lower-middle-income countries): Malaysia (upper-middle-income countries).

Source: World Bank, *World Development Indicators,* and IMF staff calculations

Figure 6-10   GDP Growth Relative to Employment Growth

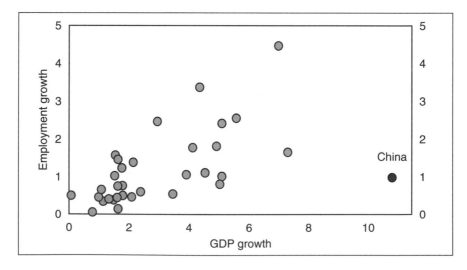

How to Address These Imbalances

There has been progress on rebalancing growth in China.

- China has made commendable progress in expanding its social safety nets in recent years. It has allocated greater resources to its pension, healthcare, and education systems since the outbreak of the financial crisis. A new government health insurance program has been launched nationwide, with the objective of achieving near-universal coverage by the end of 2012, and subsidies for a core set of prescription drugs have been introduced. On pensions, full portability of benefits has been introduced to enable greater labor mobility. The existing government pension scheme is being expanded to cover urban unemployed workers across the country by the end of 2012, while the newly introduced rural pension scheme now covers 60 percent of all counties. This should help lower precautionary savings.
- Recent trade data indicate that China's trade surplus is narrowing (see Figure 6-11), and it is likely that the surpluses will continue to fall in 2012–2013, well below what IMF staff had projected at the conclusion of the 2011 Article IV consultation (5.1 percent of GDP in 2012 and 5.25 percent of GDP in 2013). The trade surplus amounted to about US$138 billion through November, down 18 percent from the same period in 2010.
- This narrowing of the trade surplus occurred despite limited exchange-rate appreciation and was possible mainly because of deteriorating terms of trade, continued high levels of investment, and slower gains in market

Figure 6-11   Current Account and Components

(Percent of GDP)

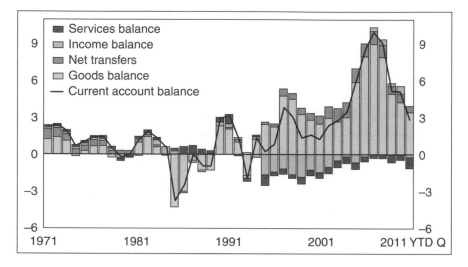

share. The slower gains in market share could in turn reflect waning benefits from China's entry into the WTO, relocation of global production capacity, and rapid productivity gains. Although these structural forces could mean a much lower medium-term current account surplus compared with IMF staff forecasts at the time of the 2011 Article IV consultation, the yuan appreciation and structural reforms put in place need to be sustained to promote a lasting rebalancing of the Chinese economy. To successfully accomplish this rebalancing and secure medium-term growth prospects, the incentive structure that guides household and corporate decisions will need to be reshaped with additional reforms to social insurance, the financial sector, and factor pricing, as well as further exchange-rate appreciation.

Additional Reforms in Healthcare, Pensions, and Education

- *Health.* Access to healthcare needs to continue to improve through training personnel and providing adequate incentives for skilled medical staff to relocate to rural areas. Further reductions in out-of-pocket expenses can be achieved through lower copays on medical procedures and drugs and more comprehensive insurance coverage for catastrophic and chronic conditions.
- *Pensions.* The complexity of rules and regulations covering the multiple national, provincial, private, and public pension programs can be simplified to encourage greater participation in pension schemes covering all categories of workers—urban, rural, and migrant.
- *Education.* More comprehensive education subsidies would ease saving impulses, particularly among young households.

Barnett and Brooks (2010) show that higher government spending on healthcare reduces urban household saving in China significantly. A 1-yuan increase in government health spending is associated with a 2-yuan increase in household consumption.

Financial-Sector Reform

In recent years, China has taken several steps toward a more market-based financial system. Bank balance sheets have been strengthened by parceling out bad loans (amounting to around 15 percent of GDP in 1999) to asset management companies, and banks have subsequently been recapitalized. The major banks have been listed on international stock exchanges, and the system has become more commercially oriented. However, the existing system of financial intermediation continues to hold back rebalancing. The use of administered deposit and lending rates combined with credit quotas favors large corporations at the expense of households and smaller service-sector firms.[7] This system of intermediation has placed the economy on a path toward excess capacity, diminishing marginal productivity of capital, and deteriorating credit quality. A continued reliance on the existing financial framework could eventually lead to a fresh wave of bank recapitalizations and additional wealth transfers from households to the banks and corporations. Such an outcome would further set back the transformation of the growth model.

Building on the steps already taken, there is a need to proceed immediately with further financial liberalization and reform. Financial reform is a lengthy and complex process that will need to be carefully guided through preemptive policy action. Starting now will ensure that the process can be largely completed during the twelfth Five Year Plan period (which runs from 2011 to 2015). If disintermediation pressures and financial innovation do set the agenda, the risk of an uncoordinated, disorderly, and chaotic reshaping of financial arrangements must be avoided by enacting adequate regulatory and supervisory oversight.

Therefore, financial liberalization should proceed with caution. Insights from other economies that have undertaken financial reforms suggest the need for a clear sequencing to minimize the risks of financial instability, undue asset prices, and macroeconomic volatility. While there is no unique, optimal path of liberalization, a possible sequencing of financial

reform laid out in the staff report for the 2011 Article IV consultation with China is as follows:

- *Liquidity absorption and the monetary framework.* With a
  stronger yuan, the People's Bank of China can absorb the
  significant excess liquidity in the system through a greater
  use of open-market operations, as the Federal Reserve
  does. With tighter liquidity conditions, monetary policy
  can begin using price-based tools such as interbank rates
  to affect the flow of credit in the economy. Essentially, the
  central bank would have more control over money and
  liquidity in the system.
- *Regulatory framework.* Regulatory and supervisory
  capability will need to be ramped up to safeguard
  financial stability as liberalization proceeds. Components
  of an enhanced regulatory framework would include
  improved monitoring and data collection, routine stress
  testing, increased oversight for systemic institutions, and
  closer interagency coordination to close the gaps in
  coverage.
- *Financial market development.* As the regulatory framework
  is strengthened, alternative channels of financial
  intermediation that reduce the reliance on banks should be
  promoted. Developing a deep and liquid fixed-income
  market that trades securities across the maturity spectrum
  with the active participation of pension funds, insurance
  companies, and mutual funds will be an essential
  objective. This will need to move in step with reforms in
  bank-based intermediation, particularly the liberalization
  of interest rates. Failure to deregulate interest rates will
  create disintermediation pressures as households seek
  higher-yielding financial investment opportunities, such

as wealth management products, outside the traditional banking system.

• *Capital controls.* With a strong regulatory framework in place, overseeing a financial system that offers a wide menu of financing and investment options, capital account liberalization could be advanced, and the yuan could be more fully internationalized. The process should start with easing restrictions on foreign direct investment and long-term flows before steadily increasing the QFII (qualified foreign institutional investors) and QDII (qualified domestic institutional investors) quotas to open up short-term portfolio flows. Eventually, the quotas should be dismantled altogether.

Input Costs and Corporate Reforms

Factor price and corporate governance reforms will shift resources away from capital-intensive sectors. If input costs were to rise closer to levels in comparable economies, and if the cost of capital were aligned with its high return, this would reduce the excess revenue earned by exporting firms and move investment toward domestically oriented sectors. The impact of these measures would be even greater if they were combined with corporate governance reforms that would extract more substantial dividend payments from large firms, in conjunction with administrative reforms that would reduce barriers to entry into the service sector.

Yuan Appreciation

The yuan has been undervalued, with clear implications for progress in other areas of reform. Pinning down the degree of undervaluation of a currency is not easy, particularly for coun-tries that are undergoing rapid structural change. However, for China there have been three main reasons to believe that the yuan has been undervalued.

- First, with an average increase of more than US$180 billion per quarter, international reserves have now reached US$3.2 trillion, well above the levels needed for precautionary purposes.
- Second, the yuan appreciated in real effective terms by about 5 ¾ percent during 2011, but, from a longer-term perspective, the yuan is in real effective terms close to where it was in the late 1990s (see Figure 6-12), despite significantly higher productivity than China's trading partners since then.

Figure 6-12 Real Effective Exchange Rate

(Index 2005 = 100; increase = appreciation)

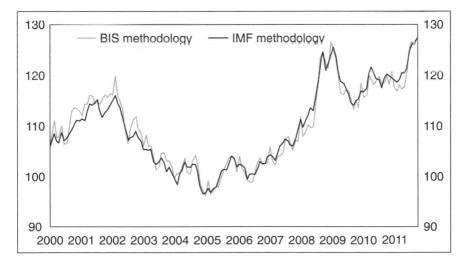

- Finally, despite important progress that has been made in many policy areas, the critical mass of measures needed to decisively change the incentives for saving and investment and achieve a lasting decline in the current account surplus is not yet in place. Indeed, simulations using the IMF multicountry model suggest that there will be pressure on China's current account surplus to rise again over the medium term, albeit to a smaller level than before the crisis (see Figure 6-13). As the global economy recovers, so will external demand for China's exports. This, together with the fiscal position moving back to budget balance and assuming a constant real effective exchange rate, means that there is a potential for somewhat larger current account surpluses to reassert themselves. The accumulation of net foreign assets will also put upward pressure on the current account surplus through its impact on income flows.

Figure 6-13 Current Account Balance
(Percent of GDP)

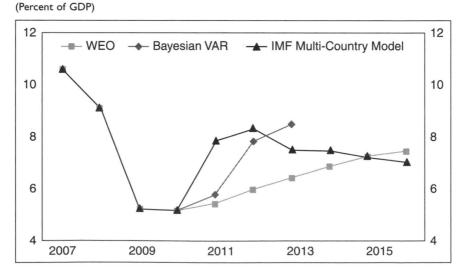

The Chinese authorities have long recognized the need to transform China's economic growth model. This concern was reflected in Premier Wen's declaration during the National People's Congress press conference in March 2007 that "the biggest problem with China's economy is that the growth is unstable, unbalanced, uncoordinated, and unsustainable." Exchange-rate appreciation is a key ingredient—and in many ways a prerequisite—for accelerating the transformation of China's economic growth model. For example, exchange-rate appreciation closer to the level consistent with medium-term fundamentals and greater flexibility will allow the central bank to run a more independent monetary policy and increase real interest rates to combat inflation pressures in a more efficient manner. At the same time, greater two-way movement of the yuan will reduce the liquidity injection needed to limit appreciation pressures and the subsequent reliance on reserve requirements and issuance of central bank paper to absorb liquidity in the domestic money market.

With higher real interest rates and less pressure on domestic liquidity from large-scale foreign exchange intervention, the government will be able to move ahead with financial-sector liberalization while avoiding the risks that financial liberalization and excess liquidity can fuel. These include the serious risks of asset price bubbles and deteriorating credit quality, culminating in a full-blown crisis. In the real sector, an undervalued exchange rate also creates distortions in relative prices that act as headwinds to the government's efforts to raise household income and to develop the service sector.

A faster pace of appreciation would open the way to move ahead with the structural reforms highlighted earlier. Moreover, a stronger yuan would help increase the purchasing power of households, raise the labor share of income, and reorient investment toward nontradable (service-oriented) sectors. Finally, a more appreciated currency would improve the potential for the yuan to be used internationally. In particular, it would reduce the risks of a one-sided use of the yuan for trade settlements, as expectations of currency appreciation would favor yuan settlement for imports at the expense of exports.

What Would Be the Benefits of Rebalancing Growth in China?

Rebalancing the economy away from exports and investment and toward consumption would have several advantages. First, it would make China less reliant on demand from its trading partners in advanced economies and less exposed to external shocks. Second, a more balanced economy—particularly with investments in social support systems and rising household income—would lessen income inequalities and increase the inclusiveness of China's growth. Finally, transforming the growth model would make China less energy- and capital-intensive and more environmentally friendly, and, over time, would add to the pace of job creation.

Nevertheless, in the near term, the shift toward domestic consumption is likely to reduce growth somewhat as the economy adjusts to the various elements of reform—in particular, because it will take some time to build productivity in the service industries. In the labor market, rebalancing will imply moving a large number of less-skilled workers from the tradable to the nontradable sector, and this process could be accompanied by short-term costs. Mitigating these costs will require labor-market policies to cushion the employment impact during the transition, particularly in meeting the skills gap that exists between workers in the tradable sector and those in the service sector.

More vigorous Chinese domestic demand would help support the global economy in many ways, including the absorption of more imports with positive spillovers to much of the rest of the world. To achieve this rebalancing, a stronger yuan will be needed as part of a comprehensive package, as it would open the way to move ahead with structural reforms, help increase the purchasing power of households, raise the labor share of income, and reorient investment toward nontradable sectors.

CHAPTER 7

CURRENCY WARS AND A GROWING ROLE FOR THE INTERNATIONAL MONETARY FUND

JAMES RICKARDS

"The role of the SDR has not been put into full play due to limitations on its allocation and the scope of its uses. However, it serves as the light in the tunnel for the reform of the international monetary system."

—Zhou Xiaochuan, People's Bank of
China Governor, March 2009

The history of the international monetary system over the past 150 years is one of relatively long periods of stability interspersed with periods of dysfunction and punctuated by abrupt changes in the prevailing rules of the game. The periods of stability are the classical gold standard period of 1870–1914, the Bretton Woods gold-backed dollar period of 1944–1971, and the strong dollar period of 1982–2010. The periods of dysfunction include the beggar-thy-neighbor devaluations of the 1920s and

1930s, beginning with the Weimar hyperinflation of 1921 and continuing through the Tripartite Agreement of 1936, called Currency War I.[1] Another period of dysfunction came in the aftermath of President Nixon's abandonment of the link between gold and the U.S. dollar in 1971, which was followed by repeated devaluations of the dollar and hyperinflation in the United States, part of what is described as Currency War II.[2]

The occasional shocks are even more dramatic than the currency wars. In 1914, nations around the world abruptly abandoned the gold standard in order to finance their participation in World War I with fiat money. In 1933, President Franklin D. Roosevelt issued an executive order suddenly ending the convertibility of dollars into gold by U.S. citizens. In 1971, President Nixon surprised the world by suspending the convertibility of dollars into gold by sovereign nations, including the United States' largest trading partners.

These alternating periods of calm and dysfunction and periodic shocks should serve as a warning to market participants that nothing is forever in the international monetary system. Despite the apparent solidity of global financial arrangements when viewed in freeze frame, the dynamic rise and fall of international currency regimes is very much the norm. The greatest danger in international currency markets is posed exactly when the system is on the brink of one of these shocks. Most market players expect more of the same and are either unaware of the danger or unprepared for the ground to shift beneath them. In this chapter, we look at some of the forces pressing on the international monetary system today and assess the chances for a once-in-a-generation shift in prevailing arrangements and the roles of the major reserve currencies—especially the U.S. dollar.

Background to a New Currency War

Currency wars are nothing more than an effort by one country to steal growth from others by devaluing its currency in order to promote exports and create jobs. Currency wars produce inflation or trade wars in the long run, but they appear to have short-run benefits that make them irresistible to politicians.

A new currency war, the third in the past century, broke out in 2010. It was most famously identified by Guido Mantega, finance minister of Brazil, who said, "We're in the midst of an international currency war" on September 27, 2010.[3] However, the new currency war had been declared even earlier by President Barack Obama in his State of the Union address on January 27, 2010, when he announced the National Export Initiative, which was intended to double U.S. exports by 2015. Although the president did not explicitly call for the devaluation of the U.S. dollar, in fact, there was no way to meet the goal of doubling exports without devaluing the dollar, since other ways of increasing exports, such as productivity increases or a greatly expanded network of free trade agreements, could not possibly work in such a short time frame.

The seeds of the new currency war had been sown even earlier, at the September 2009 summit meeting of the G-20 in Pittsburgh. At that meeting, the heads of state of 20 of the most powerful economies in the world agreed on a global growth plan under the name *rebalancing*. The intention was to rebalance elements of global growth so that Europe substituted investment for exports, China substituted consumption for exports, and the United States substituted exports for consumption. This reshuffling of the global economic deck implied a stronger euro, a stronger yuan, and a weaker dollar.

Whether this global grand bargain will play out as intended remains to be seen. However, the deal struck in Pittsburgh in 2009 and backed by Washington in early 2010 was clearly having some effects, as evidenced by the complaints from Brazil in late 2010. A new currency war had well and truly begun. As in all wars, there would be winners—and losers.

The Rise of the G-20

The two previous currency wars had been mediated through a series of conferences and agreements among the principal nations involved. These were done on an ad hoc basis with different parties at different stages, and they tended to address whatever issue was most pressing or acute at the time.

Currency War I had included the Genoa Conference of 1922, the Dawes Plan of 1924, the Young Plan of 1929, and the Tripartite Agreement of 1936. Currency War II had been mediated by the Smithsonian Agreement of 1971, the Plaza Accord of 1985, and the Louvre Accord of 1987.

The new currency war would be different. A more coherent and continuous organization was now in place in which the same participants would meet regularly, once or twice per year, to discuss the shape of the international monetary system and mediate any complaints about exchange-rate imbalances. This new organization was the G-20, which included the United States, China, Japan, Germany, France, Italy, the United Kingdom, Brazil, Russia, India, and South Korea, among others.

The G-20 had existed since 1999, but it was only in 2008, in the immediate aftermath of the collapse of Lehman Brothers and AIG and in the depths of the Panic of 2008, that the group was upgraded from a meeting for finance ministers to a leaders' summit involving heads of state. The first two G-20 summits after the panic—Washington in November 2008 and London in April 2009—were widely credited with coordinating a successful response to the global financial collapse. This response included coordinated monetary easing, information sharing, and a determination to avoid protectionism and to increase bank capital requirements.

By the time of the Pittsburgh G-20 summit in September 2009, the emphasis had turned from preventing collapse to stimulating growth. It was at Pittsburgh that the plan for rebalancing was approved, which was taken by the United States as a green light for a cheaper dollar and the appreciation of the yuan and the euro.

The role of the G-20 will become even more high profile in the years ahead as the currency wars spread. The bilateral struggle between the dollar and the yuan is sometimes carried out in two-party discussions between the United States and China nicknamed "G-2." However, many of the losers in the currency wars, such as Brazil, South Korea, and Indonesia, have no particular leverage to offset the U.S. drive for a cheap dollar and will seek to have their concerns addressed in the context of the G-20, where coalitions can be assembled to push back against the U.S. devaluation policy.

Despite the power and the visibility of the G-20, it operates with very few staff members and no permanent secretariat. At times it seems to resemble the mythical village of Brigadoon, which emerges from an empty spot on the map, only to disappear after a single day and later reemerge. In fact, preparation for each G-20 meeting and follow-up on its goals and missions goes on continuously in the separate finance ministries and central banks of the member states.

The G-20 is not without extensive technical resources. Its members have chosen to use the International Monetary Fund (IMF) as a kind of outsourced secretariat. IMF representatives attend the G-20 meetings and receive instructions for what is called "mutual assessment"—a kind of IMF report card on the progress of individual nations toward the goals agreed to at the G-20 summit. The IMF conducts these and other analyses between G-20 meetings and reports back to the G-20 in advance of the next summit as an aid to setting the agenda. The emergence of the IMF as the handmaid of the G-20 is one of the most important developments in international finance in recent years.

Reinventing the IMF

As late as 2007, experts on the international monetary system were raising serious questions about the role and future of the IMF and whether the time had come to abolish it. The IMF was created as part of the Bretton Woods Agreement in 1944, which reestablished the international monetary system after the wreckage of World War II.

The Bretton Woods system was based on a fixed exchange rate between the dollar and gold and a set of fixed exchange rates between the dollar and all other participating currencies. This meant that the other currencies had an indirect link to gold via the dollar. However, the dollar-gold relationship was the anchor of the system. It was assumed that from time to time, certain currencies might revalue relative to the dollar; however, such revaluations were expected to be rare.

What was foreseen was that certain countries might run persistent trade deficits, which would put downward pressure on their currencies. In order to maintain the peg to the dollar, those countries would have to engage in structural economic adjustments to reestablish favorable terms of trade and convert deficits into surpluses. This is not unlike the process that Greece is going through, although that process is designed to reestablish creditworthiness and solvency within the euro, since Greece does not have its own currency. However, these adjustment processes can take several years. In contrast, currency crises can drain a country's reserves in a matter of weeks or months.

The IMF was created to give countries that were experiencing currency stress time to implement their adjustment policies without running short of reserves in the meantime. The IMF would provide a kind of bridge loan from the resources of its entire membership to aid the country that was undergoing an adjustment so that it would not run out of reserves while waiting for the new policies to have the intended effects and restore the balance of trade.

This bridge loan function was rendered obsolete after 1973, when countries abandoned the Bretton Woods structure and adopted floating exchange rates. Now, instead of painful multiyear adjustment programs, countries could adjust their terms of trade immediately by allowing their currencies to devalue in the open market.

By the 1980s, the IMF had reinvented itself as a bridge lender and financial cop on the beat to emerging-market countries in Latin America, Africa, and Asia. These were countries that had not been a major part of global capital markets and currency flows during the Bretton Woods period, but that were now becoming more important as trading partners for sellers of manufactured goods and buyers of natural resources.

This new role for the IMF ended disastrously during the Asian financial crisis of 1997–1998. When the worst-affected countries, such as Thailand, Malaysia, Indonesia, and South Korea, needed financial assistance to fight off a wholesale flight of hot money out of their banking systems, the IMF provided resources, but it also imposed austerity plans that were entirely unsuitable for what were potentially fast-growing, export-driven economies. The IMF applied a remedy that was more suitable for a solvency crisis when its clients were actually facing a short-term liquidity crisis. The result was worsening economies, riots, destruction, and death in the streets.

By the early 2000s, the IMF had lost its original function among the advanced economies and had terribly mishandled its adopted function among the emerging economies. It seemed to have no role and no future. This changed radically with the Panic of 2008.

Suddenly the world needed a financial cop, think tank, enforcer, and proto-central bank all at once. Despite its poor performance in the late 1990s, the IMF did have a large, highly regarded staff of experts along with a global membership, a governance structure, a budget, and a massive database. While the G-20 had power, the IMF had all of the other things that the G-20 lacked in the way of structure and resources. This institutional legacy proved decisive in helping the IMF to survive and find a new mission.

By 2009, the G-20 had "adopted" the IMF as its eyes and ears to monitor developments in the international monetary system along with progress toward stated G-20 goals. The IMF performed these functions at the request of the G-20, but it did so using its own techniques and staff, and therefore gained a measure of autonomy in the global economic rebalancing process.

This role as the expert mediator and monitor of the international monetary system was just the beginning of the emergence of a new, more powerful IMF, albeit under the direction of the G-20. By early 2011, the IMF was taking concrete steps to establish itself as a world central bank that was capable of issuing its own world money—the Special Drawing Right (SDR).

A New World Currency

The most salient developments in the international monetary system for the foreseeable future will involve the decline in the status of the dollar as the world's leading reserve currency. Decline does not mean collapse or elimination. It means a diminution in the dollar's percentage of total global reserves, along with a diminution in the power and influence that come with being the dominant reserve currency.

In 2000, the U.S. dollar made up 71 percent of all identified foreign exchange reserves in the world.[4] By the end of 2011, the U.S. dollar component of identified foreign exchange reserves had dropped to 62 percent.[5] Over the same period, the absolute size of identified U.S. dollar reserves had increased from approximately $1.1 trillion to $3.4 trillion, a 300 percent increase. However, other currencies, such as the euro, yen, Swiss franc, and pound sterling, had increased even more, leading to a percentage decline in the U.S. dollar component and an increase in the others.

A simple extrapolation of these trends suggests a world in which the dollar drops below the 50 percent threshold and the euro and other currencies increase their shares until there is no dominant reserve currency, but rather a group of currencies, all vying for a place in the reserve accounts of the world's central banks and sovereign wealth funds. This could happen in as little as 10 years, perhaps sooner.

This world of multiple reserve currencies is viewed benignly by some. It seems to take the pressure off the U.S. dollar to maintain itself as a store of value. Like a dowager who is no longer vibrant but maintains some dignity, the dollar would have an important place in world finance, but it would no longer be an instrument of a robust foreign or military policy because of the prevalence of alternatives.

The leading advocate for this outcome is Berkeley professor Barry Eichengreen, who compares it to a time in the 1920s when the dollar and the pound sterling traded places as the two leading reserve currencies, with neither one completely dominant.[6] However, Eichengreen's complacency ignores the fact that the international monetary system of the 1920s was anchored by a type of gold standard—albeit the flawed gold exchange standard devised at the Genoa Conference—and that until recently, the international monetary system was at least nominally anchored in a kind of dollar standard. A world of multiple reserve currencies without gold would leave the world with no anchor at all for the first time since the creation of the Bank of England in 1694. Far from being a resolution of the currency wars, the world of multiple reserve currencies could exacerbate them, with repeated rounds of sequential devaluation by central banks and nowhere for reserve holders to take refuge.

More likely than multiple reserve currencies is a world with a single reserve currency—but not the dollar. The new king of the hill would be the SDR issued by the IMF. The IMF has already announced plans for the emergence of the SDR as the new world reserve currency.[7] These plans include an annual issuance of $200 billion equivalent in SDRs per year as well as recommendations for private SDR bond issuers, suggested SDR investors, the creation of a network of SDR dealers, and

the use of SDR repo facilities and SDR derivatives for financing and hedging purposes. In short, the SDR would be
endowed with all of the elements of a modern liquid bond
market. It is the existence of deep liquid bond markets denominated in a particular currency that is the sine qua non of
reserve currency status and distinguishes a reserve currency
from the more common trade currency.

This plan will also require years to implement, but the first
tentative steps are already being taken. For the first time in
its history, the IMF is funding its commitments on a large
scale with debt instruments rather than with equitylike member quotas. These new SDR notes are being issued to members in large quantities to fund bailouts in Europe and
elsewhere. In addition, the IMF issued approximately $294
billion in new SDRs to its members in September 2009—the
first such issuance since 1981 and by far the largest.[8]

The IMF now exhibits the combination of a leveraged balance sheet through SDR note issuance and the capacity to print
money through the recent allocations of SDRs to its members.
Combining an expanded balance sheet with money-printing
capability makes the IMF a de facto global central bank of issue
operating under G-20 auspices.

This does not mean that local currencies will perform no role
or will disappear. Currencies such as the dollar will still be
used for local transactions inside the United States in the same
way that Turkish lira are used for transactions inside Turkey
today. However, the SDR will be the exclusive unit of account
for all important international transactions, such as reserve balances, balance of payments adjustments, invoicing oil and
other global commodities, and the financial statements of the
1,000 or so largest global corporations.

Hoping for the Best—Thinking About the Worst

Given the weak dollar policies of the Obama administration and the Federal Reserve under Chairman Bernanke, the evolution of the international monetary system away from a dollar standard toward the new SDR standard seems inevitable, perhaps with a stop in the world of multiple reserve currencies during the transition. Given the many elements required for a true SDR-based system—bond issuers, investors, dealers, repo markets, derivatives, and so on—it seems that this transition will take at least five years and more likely ten or fifteen years to complete.

However, this process could be accelerated greatly in the event of another financial panic as bad as, or even worse than, the Panic of 2008. The world avoided an even greater collapse at that time through the creation of trillions of dollars of new money by all of the world's major central banks, most prominently the U.S. Federal Reserve. As a result, central bank balance sheets today are overleveraged and relatively illiquid by historical standards. Even minor interest-rate increases would wipe out all central bank capital if assets were marked to market to reflect the decline in their market value as a result of such increases. In short, the ability of central banks to duplicate the flood of liquidity they created in 2008–2010 in the event of a new financial panic is severely constrained.

Instead, the next financial panic will be addressed with liquidity not from the central banks, but from the IMF in the form of massive printing of SDRs. In such a panic, the IMF will have the only unimpaired balance sheet in the world and will therefore be the sole source of new global liquidity. This flooding of the world with new SDR liquidity, perhaps on the order of $3 trillion or more, could be the catalyst that thrusts the SDR into the role of world reserve currency ahead of schedule. While panics are by their nature impossible to predict in terms of their exact timing, it does seem more likely than not that such a scenario could play out in the next several years, considering that the problems of the 2008 collapse were never fully resolved and are still with us, buried in the balance sheets of the too-big-to-fail banks.

In the event that such a dire outcome emerges, we can at least take comfort from the fact that the G-20-IMF-SDR blueprint already exists and that the plumbing has been tested over the course of 2009–2012 with modest issuance of new SDRs and SDR notes. Executive orders would replace legislative processes in extremis, and the transition away from dollars and toward SDRs could happen quite quickly. Whether citizens of the affected nations will be content with nondemocratic processes and a new form of paper money to replace the old paper money is a question looming over all such scenarios.

When all else fails, possibly including a new SDR plan, gold is always waiting in the wings as a stable, widely accepted store of value and universal money. In the end, a global struggle between gold and SDRs for supremacy as "money" may be the next great shock added to the long list of historic shocks to the international monetary system.

CHAPTER 8

A ROLE FOR GOLD

PETER BOOCKVAR

"The system should also consider employing gold as an international reference point of market expectations about inflation, deflation and future currency values."

Robert Zoellick, former president,
World Bank, November 2010

Whether it is considered to be jewelry, money, a collectible, or just Au 79 on the periodic table, the known history of gold dates back to around 4000 BC. It's because of this longevity and because of gold's sustainability in many aspects of economic life all over the world that its importance and uses must be correctly understood. Of late, with the price of gold rising for 11 straight years after 20 years of falling prices and reaching record highs, its context and relevance today are again major topics of discussion and debate. Why has a metal that has very little industrial use stood the true test of time? Why has gold historically been found to form the backbone of entire currency regimes? Why has a metal that yields no interest income produced such incredible demand from people who are willing to give up income in paper money in return for a shiny artifact?

Also, is gold so pretty that for thousands of years, people the world over have clamored over its visuals?

While certain pieces of gold jewelry dating back past 4000 BC have been discovered over the past 40 years, it wasn't until around 2500 BC that goldsmiths in Mesopotamia (making up modern-day Iraq and parts of Syria) started to hone their craft. Fast-forward 1000 years, and gold was a predominant feature in the funeral mask of Tutankhamen. It was also around this time (1500 BC) that the world's first gold standard was unofficially established in Babylon with Egyptian-sourced gold. There were no official gold coins as a method of payment for goods, but instead spiral rings of gold were used.[1] It wasn't until 564 BC that the first official gold and silver coins came into existence during the reign of King Croesus of Lydia (part of Turkey), according to the World Gold Council.

Centuries later, the once-great Roman Empire used gold and silver coins as a core element of its monetary exchange. The Romans didn't mine the gold themselves, but rather acquired it through conquest. The span of their empire "established the first really international economy, broader even than that encompassed by today's Euro. For the legionnaires were paid in hard cash, gold and silver coin, bearing the portrait of their emperor."[2] "The normal use of coin as a means of exchange was ubiquitous ... that is to say that coin was used both in towns and in areas of settled agriculture, and in the 'less developed' as well as the 'more sophisticated' provinces. ... Money was embedded in the structure of the economy."[3] In Pompeii alone, 13,000 gold coins were found in the aftermath of the volcanic destruction of the city.[4]

For centuries to come, gold and silver coins of differing forms and weights became a standard medium of exchange, with the Roman aureus, the Byzantine nomisma, the Islamic

dinar, and the Venetian ducat being the most widely internationally accepted currencies. These were eventually followed
by the British sovereign, which was launched in 1817.[5] A corollary of the widespread expansion of coins was differing gold
standards that set the price of money at various weights
and values of gold and, for a while, silver. Over the last few
hundred years, gold physically backed certain paper money
currency regimes.

Of lesser importance to the gold market, but still representing a steady demand up to the present, is the use of gold for
industrial purposes. Dentistry, electronics, and healthcare products are just some of the industries that utilize gold. The World
Gold Council (WGC) estimates that for at least the past five
decades, technological uses of gold have made up about 10 percent of its demand, with jewelry and investment making up the
balance with about 60 percent and 30 percent, respectively.

In order to sustain any type of gold monetary exchange and
standard, and also to meet the consistent jewelry and industrial
demands, there has been a constant need and desire to find new
gold; this quest reached the shores of the United States with a
fervor during the great California gold rush, which began in
1848. Over the following few years, about 300,000 people from
all over the world migrated to California in search of riches.
With new mining techniques, gold exploration also flourished
in other parts of the world, and production skyrocketed. However, instead of collapsing as a result of the enormous increase
in supply, the price of gold remained relatively stable, as the
demand for it also continued to increase, while demand for silver declined. Today there are 165,000 metric tons of gold that
have been extracted from the ground, according to the WGC.
That is only enough to fill two Olympic-size swimming pools,
illustrating gold's status as a precious metal.

Against the backdrop of this very brief history of gold as a valuable commodity, the main purpose of this chapter, and certainly the focus of a current topic of conversation on the worldwide monetary stage, is to discuss whether gold is money, and why, given its limited industrial use and its popularity being subject to fashion trends, this valuable resource is in such great investment demand, both from individuals and, once again, from nations. In our contemporary fiat currency world, in which money is backed by nothing more than a government's word, it has suddenly become intriguing to look backward to past regimes that established gold standards in order to ascertain the real value of gold in our modern world.

The form of money that the world knows now is paper. While the paper itself is worth very little (unlike a gold coin, which has inherent value), the various denominations of paper currency determine its worth in terms of exchange. Until 1971, when the United States and most of the rest of the world relinquished the last vestige of a gold standard and paper money became fiat, paper money was usually backed by something. Governments promised to exchange paper money for a fixed amount of gold or silver at a time of the holder's choosing. Thus, paper money was collateralized. This collateral imposed a sense of discipline on those countries that printed their own currency, whether by individual banks providing notes or through a central bank that printed all of a nation's money. The amount of money printed had to have a fixed relationship with an amount of gold and/or silver held in reserve. This would prevent excessive printing of money that would inevitably devalue the stock of existing paper currency.

Even during historical periods when gold standards were in effect, they were temporarily suspended in times of war so that countries without enough tax revenue would be able to finance their military operations by printing money without restraint. The British government temporarily suspended its gold standard during the battle against Napoleon's armies in the early part of the nineteenth century. The United States did so during its Civil War in the 1860s, and many countries did so during World War I. Because most countries quickly returned to their gold standard after a war, the inflation that had flared during the war moderated.

The most glaring example of negative consequences that resulted from suspension of a gold standard and failing to reinstate it occurred in Germany during the Weimar Republic. After World War I, the new German government, in part because of reparations payments required by the Treaty of Versailles, and also in an effort to rebuild its economy, printed and printed and printed money to make payments. The value of a German mark in early 1921 was 60 to the U.S. dollar. By the end of 1922, it was 8,000. By 1923, a pound of bread cost 3 billion marks. Inevitably, the currency was revalued with a new one that eliminated most zeros, and a new form of a gold standard was reintroduced. It was this experience with hyperinflation that has embedded within the Germans a strict and unwavering commitment to sound money policy to this day.

Most recently, hyperinflation overtook Zimbabwe, where a government-wrecked economy resorted to printing money to cover up its ills. Instead, doing so further destroyed the economy by creating an inflation rate in the millions. Rather than halting the government policy responsible for the currency debasement, the central bank of Zimbabwe kept printing more money. Eventually, Zimbabwe's currency became wallpaper, and its economy switched to the U.S. dollar. The examples of Germany and Zimbabwe are extreme in terms of fiscal and monetary policies that led to hyperinflation, but the underlying theme of both stories is the presence of an unrestrained central bank that prints money at will, as dictated by its own opinions.

The modern-day discussion on gold really dates back to the Great Depression in the United States, when, some people believe, the gold standard tied the hands of central banks and deterred them from increasing the money supply and liquefying the banking system, which was under major strain at the time. These people argue that easier money would have been the key to relieving the economic stresses that resulted from the constriction in bank lending caused, in part, by many banks failing. The irony in relying on the Federal Reserve to fix the ills of a lack of liquidity in the 1930s is that its easy money policy of the mid-1920s ultimately led to the bubble of the late 1920s that was followed by the stock market crash of 1929 and the consequent tribulations of the 1930s.

In 1933, looking to the Federal Reserve for monetary help, President Franklin Delano Roosevelt signed Executive Order 6102 in order to remove its gold standard anchor. It wasn't much of an anchor, however, as James Grant once referred to the gold exchange standard of the time as being "almost as deeply flawed as the post 1971 paper dollar system," as the quantity of money grew far above any equal backing in gold. The Executive Order forbade "the hoarding of gold coin, gold bullion, and gold certificates within the continental United States." All citizens were thus ordered to sell their personal holdings of gold to the Federal Reserve for $20.67 per troy ounce. Imagine that! The U.S. government made it a criminal offense to own gold! In 1934, the Gold Reserve Act followed, forcing the Federal Reserve to turn over the gold it held to the U.S. Treasury, and soon thereafter, gold was revalued at $35 a troy ounce. It was a few years after this that England, where the pound had been considered the world's reserve currency for most of the nineteenth century, sold down much of its gold holdings in preparing for World War II and faced the realization that a proper gold standard was going to be difficult to achieve, as the war effort would require the printing of more money than there was gold to back it up.

Whatever benefits FDR and his administration were trying to achieve with this newfound freedom to lift the U.S. economy from the depths of the Depression in 1933, the reality is that it wasn't until at least 12 years later, after the end of World War II, that the U.S. economy finally got back on a firm footing. At this point, of course, industrial competition from Europe and Japan had disappeared, and U.S. business and Washington, DC, had finally made peace after FDR had vilified American industrialists during the 1930s.

John Maynard Keynes, one of the preeminent economists of the time, had influenced FDR's economic policies, promoting the theory that inflation was needed both to pay off excessive debts with devalued dollars and to raise employment. Unrestrained printing of money was certainly not free, however. Although Keynes's economic philosophies are still widely followed and implemented politically today, the results can be specious. Keynes himself said the following in his 1919 book, *The Economic Consequences of the Peace*, on the subject of a central bank free from the shackles of a gold standard:

> *Lenin is said to have declared that the best way to destroy the Capitalist System was to debauch the currency. By a continuing process of inflation, governments can confiscate, secretly and unobserved, an important part of the wealth of their citizens. By this method they not only confiscate, but they confiscate arbitrarily; and, while the process impoverishes many, it actually enriches some. ... Lenin was certainly right. There is no subtler,*

no surer means of overturning the existing basis of society than to debauch the currency. The process engages all the hidden forces of economic law on the side of destruction, and does it in a manner which not one man in a million is able to diagnose.[6]

Notwithstanding this realization, Keynes termed gold a "barbarous relic" in 1923, because of his belief that the gold standard was dead after World War I. In his mind, it was good riddance. He wanted countries to have the ability to print money at will in order to foster growth, irrespective of the inflationary pressures that would follow. Nominal (real + inflation) GDP growth was his preferred cure for economic recessions.

While he acknowledged the evils of currency debasement and inflation, Keynes was more focused on the short-term economic consequences of economic downturns. He favored both using interventionist fiscal and monetary policies to lift aggregate demand and depreciating one's currency to boost trade. While these measures would foster economic growth in the short term, the long-term consequences and "payback" were not his focus.

The wartime period during which many countries remained off the gold standard lasted until 1944, when the final remnant of a gold standard was codified in the Bretton Woods Agreement in 1944, just as World War II was nearing its end. The purpose of the Bretton Woods Agreement was to establish the U.S. dollar as the global reserve currency, enabling foreign countries to sell their dollars at will for a fixed amount of gold, since the U.S. dollar was backed by gold. The goal of this fixed currency regime was to provide stability for those countries that chose to tie and fix their currencies to the value of the U.S. dollar, this would assure a necessary degree of certainty as economic globalization started to regenerate after the war.

This attempt at an international financial system was meant to break down barriers to trade and provide the basis for a healthier and freer global economic backdrop, which would benefit all those who took part. Also, utilizing the U.S. dollar as the center of this new system would prevent other countries from manipulating their currencies at will, since at the same time that participating countries fixed their currencies to the U.S. dollar, the U.S. dollar was fixed at a value of $35 per troy ounce of gold. The Bretton Woods Agreement produced a new financial system that represented the first international agreement on monetary policy of the modern age. It remained in effect until August 1971, when President Nixon unilaterally ended this pseudo-gold standard and declared that currencies were now meant to float, without the constraint of any ties to gold. Because many nations had pegged their own currencies to the U.S. dollar, which was now no longer linked to gold, a global freely floating currency regime was, in essence, created.

A new fiat currency regime was established because the United States found it increasingly difficult to sustain a peg to gold, in part because of fiscal policies used to finance the Vietnam War and the Great Society spending initiatives of the 1960s. These had included the use of borrowed money instead of tax revenue for funding. Foreigners, seeing the flood of U.S. dollars, wanted gold instead, forcing Nixon to eventually put a stop to the convertibility of the U.S. dollar into gold. This allowed gold itself to start to trade, and it flew upward from the $35 level.

With currencies now floating freely in relation to one another without the anchor of gold, it was left to the fiscal and monetary policies of individual nations to determine the value of their currency in the internationally traded markets. What soon followed, as the decade of the 1970s progressed, was a major inflation problem, with the rate of consumer price inflation in the United States in particular reaching 13.5 percent year over year in 1980. Gold topped out at $850 per troy ounce in 1980, when the U.S. Federal Reserve finally used the lever of interest rates to tighten money to such an extent that it quelled the inflation of money creation. The immediate slowdown in economic activity that resulted led to a sharp fall in the rate of change in consumer prices over the subsequent years.

The much more benign growth in the rate of inflation that lasted over the next 20 years ultimately led the price of gold to fall to as low as $250 per troy ounce in 1999. The purchasing power of the dollars in your pocket still went down, but at a pace that was dramatically lower than that seen in the 1970s. U.S. central bankers had succeeded in creating their own "gold standard" by implementing policies that provided price stability; it seemed as though they had created a basis for healthy, unrestrained economic growth. And so they believed.

Any discussion of gold and its proper worth cannot be detached from a study of the actions of the U.S. Federal Reserve and other central banks in the world, such as the European Central Bank, the Bank of England, and the Bank of Japan. As gold is a currency and not a commodity, its value is directly related to the market's perception of its competition with paper currencies, whose supply is dictated by central banks and the fiscal policies of individual governments. The value of a currency is very simply determined by the supply of it relative to the demand. Economics 101 taught some of us that a greater supply of a good compared with the demand for it would result in a lower price, and vice versa. Every day, $4 trillion worth of foreign currencies are traded, and market participants' opinions of supply and demand are put to the test. The supply of gold, however, is not determined by the whims of politicians and central bankers. Its supply is determined solely by the ability to mine it from the ground. Thus its price is determined strictly by its availability from mines and the desire to sell it at a profit. Consequently, it is this independence from politics and government intervention in the marketplace that has set gold in its place as a valuation benchmark for fiat currencies.

To visualize monetary policy without the constraints of a gold standard, one must realize that in the short term, the cost of money is determined by men and women seated around large tables in their respective central bank conference rooms. Using econometric models and forecasts, they are all trying to pick the "right" interest rate. That "right" rate, of course, varies based on the individual circumstances of each of their countries, but my point is that this arbitrary conduct of policy is prone to danger. Compare this scenario to the setting of interest rates in the marketplace, where millions of participants decide at what price they want to lend money, and others decide at what price they are willing to borrow. The market gets it wrong sometimes, but the beauty of the market is that it quickly readjusts when it goes wrong. Bureaucrats in elaborate offices aren't that quick to adjust, and they often purposely choose to manipulate the cost of money to achieve a particular level of economic performance that they are determined to achieve.

We need look no further than the U.S. economy over the past 10 years and the actions of our central bank to see what can go wrong when one ignores the price of gold, and instead has too much faith in a crystal ball. Following the easy money–induced stock market bubble in the United States in the late 1990s, which resulted in a major bust, Alan Greenspan, Ben Bernanke, and Co. cut the fed funds rate from 6.5 percent to 1 percent and maintained that level for years, irrespective of the rising level of inflation, because they wanted to juice economic growth through the extension of credit.

This cheapening of money led to the greatest credit bubble this world has ever seen, and we're currently still dealing with the aftermath. The Bernanke-led Fed embarked on multiple rounds of interest-rate cuts and money printing, known as quantitative easing (QE), in order to price-fix the cost of money lower. But instead of facilitating years of needed deleveraging, the Fed has been trying to put Humpty Dumpty back together again, and, in the process, has tried to repair an economy that is characterized by too much personal borrowing, too little saving, and too much spending. I emphasize this because it directly relates to the value of gold, as the Fed is creating money out of thin air in order to achieve its monetary goals. It thus goes back to Economics 101, where we learned that too great a supply of currency relative to the demand for it cheapens the currency, and inversely, that is increasingly seen in the price of gold. The price level of gold is the best measure of this imbalance, as the supply of gold can't be created by the Fed.

Over the past few years, attempts to inflate one's way out of an overindebted economy have occurred in England, Japan, and most of Europe. Switzerland has taken part in its own form of money printing; however, this has been more focused on fixing the value of the Swiss franc to the euro. Most of the Western world is suffering from a lack of growth and extraordinary levels of debt. Instead of encouraging healthy growth through long-term policies and debt paydown and writedown, central banks are trying to prevent, at all costs, any sort of needed adjustments by employing massive liquidity steps, resulting in a debasement of currencies as the creation of money is inflated on a grand scale.

Figures 8-1 to 8-3 show the respective balance sheets of the European Central Bank, the Fed, and the Bank of England.

Ironically, it is the central banks in developing countries that have added to their gold reserves in order to protect themselves

Figure 8-1   ECB in Euros

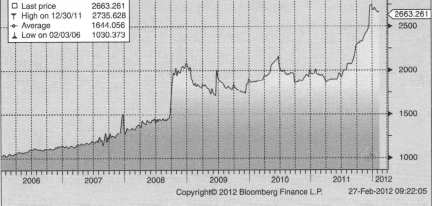

□ Last price	2663.261
⊤ High on 12/30/11	2735.628
⊸ Average	1644.056
⊥ Low on 02/03/06	1030.373

Figure 8-2   Federal Reserve in U.S. Dollars

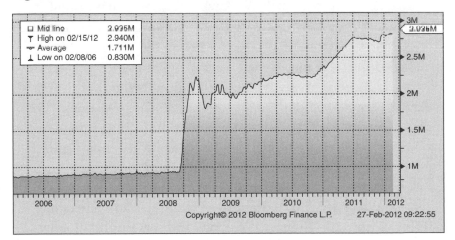

□ Mid line	2.935M
⊤ High on 02/15/12	2.940M
⊸ Average	1.711M
⊥ Low on 02/08/06	0.830M

Figure 8-3 Bank of England in pounds

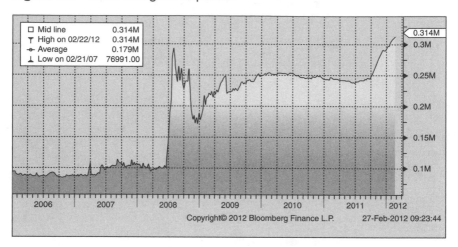

and their U.S. dollar, euro, and yen holdings from debasement. According to the World Gold Council, in the first three months of 2011, central banks bought a net 350 tons of gold, and 148.4 tons in the third quarter alone. This compares to a net 180 tons bought in 1988, the last time central banks were net buyers. While there is no official breakdown of which countries bought gold, Russia, Thailand, Bolivia, Brazil, and Mexico have publicly stated that they have added to their holdings. These central banks are not speculating on higher prices; they are structurally changing the asset mix of their reserve holdings.

In the absence of any type of restraint, whether political or through a gold standard or something similar to it, unelected central bankers have run rampant over an international economic system that was once dependent on the free flow of goods and services, with the cost of money being determined mostly by the marketplace at a level above the rate of inflation. As in any bubble, a misallocation of capital results from a muddying of the price discovery of goods and services that follows an inaccurate measure of the pricing of credit. For example, artificially cheap money created by the Fed in the mid-2000s led to excessive credit demand that manifested itself in the housing market, creating a level of housing prices that was, in turn, artificial. Rising prices attracted even more capital, and the obvious bubble resulted. If there is any indictment of central bank policy, specifically that of the U.S. Federal Reserve, it is the current economic malaise, the debt overhang, and the price of gold. The price of gold is directly tied to the value of the alternative fiat currencies, and the 11-year bull market in gold to an all-time record high in August of 2011 fully expressed the market's view of the reckless fiscal and monetary policy being conducted by our elected and unelected officials and their impact on paper money.

Figure 8-4 is a chart of the Consumer Price Index, in which we can see a notable increase beginning in 1971, just as the handcuffs of a gold standard were lifted from central bankers. Price stability this is not—and it's the standard of living of the

Figure 8-4 Consumer Price Index

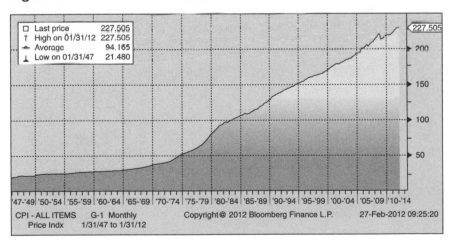

□	Last price	227.505
↑	High on 01/31/12	227.505
◆	Average	94.165
⊥	Low on 01/31/47	21.480

CPI - ALL ITEMS   G-1 Monthly   Copyright@ 2012 Bloomberg Finance L.P.   27-Feb-2012 09:25:20
    Price Indx   1/31/47 to 1/31/12

middle class that gets destroyed. The purchasing power of the U.S. dollar has declined 82.5 percent since 1971 and 94 percent since 1934, when FDR altered its value versus gold. Income inequality is now a huge debate, but where is the criticism of the Fed for perpetuating it? One of the Fed's publicly stated goals is a rise in asset prices as a result of its policies, but only half of Americans own assets. Inflation is the Fed's unspoken goal—but many people can't handle it because their wages can't keep up. Gold was once a check on the behavior of central bankers, but fortunately (and unfortunately), we are now gaining a body of evidence concerning the damage that is done when the discipline is not there. Some examples are reflected in Figures 8-4 and 8-5, the cost of living (CPI) and the amount of debt the U.S. federal government (not even including state and local debt) has accumulated over the years.

While gold may not mean much to those who don't wear it as jewelry or use it for some industrial purpose, it has a history of serving as a form of money, a means of exchange, and a store

Figure 8-5   U.S. Total Treasury Public Debt Outstanding

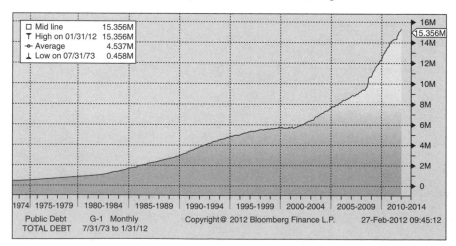

of value for thousands of years. Its price is determined solely by the supply of it that has been taken out of the ground relative to the demand for it, and more and more of the demand for gold over the past 10 years has been from investors. Every single central banker should ask himself (or herself), "Why on earth would an investor buy a metal that yields nothing and can't be used as a form of exchange to buy even a pack of gum at the local convenience store?" What they don't realize is that gold represents a form of protection: protection of the value of one's hard-earned income, protection against inflation, and thus protection against the incompetence of a set of men and women who are wrongly entrusted with picking the right borrowing rate and protection against elected officials who spend money that they don't have and never plan to repay with currency with the same value as that which was borrowed.

Congressman Ron Paul once asked Ben Bernanke whether gold was money, and the chairman of our Federal Reserve responded, "No." Coming from a supposed historian of economics, that should alarm the rest of us who understand gold's place in history. Gold is not held because of longstanding tradition, as Bernanke believes; ironically, it's held as a form of self-defense against policy makers such as him. We are fast approaching another form of a gold standard, whether backed by gold itself or by silver or a basket of commodities. The bond market in Europe has revolted against excessive debt caused by reckless spending and anemic growth, and it is naïve to think that this trend won't make its way to Japan, the United Kingdom, and eventually the shores of the United States, as all suffer from the same characteristics. Not until the printing press is finally taken away from the Fed and other central bankers the world over will the economies of the developed world be back on a stable, less leveraged foundation.

In the current state of currencies that float freely against one another, gold will be the last man standing in terms of a store of value and the maintenance of purchasing power that is derived from this. No central banker can create it or print it, as its supply is limited to what can be found in the ground. We have all seen firsthand what unrestrained central bankers can do to their currency and their economy. Irrespective of their good intentions, central bank policies create booms and busts, with economic repercussions that damage the lives of many. Also, the constant reduction of the purchasing power of paper currencies via inflation as a result of excessive money printing reduces the standard of living of those who can least afford it.

Free markets don't need fine tuning of monetary policy to create a temporary, yet false, sense of security; they can adjust on their own to the inevitable dislocations that always occur and that are healthy in cleansing the economic system of any excess. Gold, and a currency standard backed by it or something like it, puts handcuffs on central bankers and creates a certain level of restraint in their actions that limits their constant intervention in a free-market economy, the clear repercussions of which are distortion, manipulation, currency debasement, and asset bubbles and crashes.

CHINA

ROBERT JOHNSON

"When large economies with undervalued exchange rates act to keep the currency from appreciating, that encourages other countries to do the same. This sets off a dangerous dynamic."
—Tim Geithner, October 2010

Currency imbalances in the global economy played an integral part in creating the 2008 financial crisis. The old Bretton Woods system devised after World War II, which broke down in 1971, has not been replaced by a monetary system that is capable of dealing with the problems of today's volatile currency markets and trade imbalances. Given this, China's unilateral currency peg will not work going forward. China is simply too large a country to continue on the mercantilist path of export-led growth. Threats of protectionism, a paradox of risk aversion, and the specter of a worldwide recession will loom as long as China continues in this direction. If the world's leading nations, now including China, are unable to collectively find a way forward, the future of the world economy looks dim. There are strong financial interests on all sides, domestic and international. The outcome of their struggles will determine what comes next. This article examines the present imbalances that have resulted from China's peg and suggests possible futures for its currency policy as it relates to both domestic issues and foreign policy.

The world is out of balance.

In the West, a sovereign debt crisis is looming, with troubled developed countries being politically unable to restructure their debt or create long-term programs to pull themselves out of downward spirals exacerbated by a series of international austerity frenzies. The U.S. government, in the aftermath of a brutal financial collapse, is squabbling over tax cuts for the wealthy. Meanwhile, the European Union has been incapable of resolving its core structural problems, and its democratic governments are once again proving incapable of facing the collective challenges of a systemic economic crisis. The rituals of austerity that we've seen in the United States and Europe— ill-fated attempts to spur growth in depressed economies by contracting the public sector—would be familiar to any scholar of the early twentieth century and the Great Depression. Indeed, the global economy is beginning to exhibit symptoms similar to those of the 1920s and 1930s, except with a modern twist. Today, the world is suffering the consequences of having its stability and growth tied to the U.S. economy and of Europe's failure to emerge as a viable alternative to America's economic strength.

Through this dysfunction, China has experienced a meteoric rise. In just a few decades, China has become the world's second largest economy and its largest export economy. And it won't be long before China passes the United States to become the biggest overall economy on earth. The International Monetary Fund (IMF), for instance, estimates that by 2016, China will have the world's largest gross domestic product (GDP).[1]

What's all the more remarkable is that China has managed to achieve this unprecedented growth even amidst a global economic crisis. In 2010, its GDP rose an estimated 10.328 percent.[2] By comparison, U.S. GDP over the same period grew by just 2.8 percent.

On the surface, China's growing influence is not dissimilar to America's emergence in the late nineteenth and early twentieth centuries at the expense of Great Britain, the dominant power at the time. However, as you start peeling back the layers of China's economy, those similarities fall apart.

First and foremost, the magnitude of China's size and scale is unmatched in recent history. Based on this alone, China commands the world's attention. But second, and possibly more importantly, China is the first true world power to have achieved its international status before it has approached anything approximating economic parity with the current world leaders. This is essential to understanding why it will be so much more difficult for society to integrate China as a leader of the global economic system than it was to handle the transition in power from Britain to the United States.

In many ways, China is still a desperately poor country. Despite its rampant growth, its GDP per capita in 2011 was around 16 percent of that of the United States.[3] Furthermore, much of China's population remains at near-subsistence levels, and the country has yet to establish a true middle class whose consumption can sustain a domestic demand–led economy. China's economy remains thoroughly export-driven, and this trend is likely to continue into the near future. China's consumer demand will not grow fast enough in the short term to make up for the decrease in consumer demand from developed countries, particularly the United States. It will take many years before developing countries see private consumption in China replace investment as the key driver of economic growth. The countries that will benefit from China's investment will largely be those that are rich in the natural resources that China requires in increasing amounts to continue its growth and development.[4] So while China's economy is catching up to the developed world, its growth cannot become the locomotive that tows developed nations out of their slump.

In fact, China's current economic policies appear to be hurting the economic growth of the developed world, particularly the United States. Given the wide disparities in wealth, technology, and resources, China has been able to achieve its success in large part by preventing its currency, the renminbi (RMB), also known as the yuan, from appreciating against the dollar. This enables Chinese exporters to be ultracompetitive in the global market and keeps the American and European economies vulnerable to the deflationary impact of a growing low-cost Chinese manufacturing base.

China's insistence on using a peg for its currency is very uncharacteristic for leaders in the global economy, which typically allow their currencies to float because the world needs a multilateral system. But China has refused to set its currency free. While this strategy may have accelerated China's growth, it also has created dire consequences throughout the world, especially in the United States. The country's RMB currency peg may have produced massive trade surpluses for China, but it also contributed to similarly large trade deficits for the United States. America's current account and global merchandise trade deficits peaked in 2006 at a staggering $857 billion, or 6.5 percent of GDP,[5] though by 2010 this deficit had declined to $470 billion, or 3 percent of GDP, as a result of the recession.[6]

China's currency peg has also been shown to contribute to increased income inequality in the United States.[7] Not only does a pegged RMB suppress wages in the U.S. manufacturing sector, but it also leads to rising unemployment and increased use of transfer payments (government sepending on unemployment compensation and various social benefit programs).[8] China's development is, in effect, imposing severe adjustment strains on the developed countries by overtly exporting unemployment to those countries, particularly the United States. In an era of deficient consumer demand, China's policy has contributed to a sharp decline in household income in the United States in areas affected by the loss of manufacturing jobs because of exposure to Chinese imports.[9] Overall, China's pegged currency has accelerated the hollowing out of the American middle class—the very same middle class that Chinese exporters have long depended on to fuel their growth.

For decades, the United States has served as a buyer of last resort for goods produced by the rest of the world. During this time, the United States has also gone from being the world's leading net exporter to being the world's leading net importer. What's more, the United States' rapacious consumer demand has helped create a situation in which the three largest economies after the United States are all export-led. Throughout the twentieth century, developed countries found success by exporting goods to feed the U.S. consumer engine. As a result of this international trade structure, the global economy has become increasingly dependent on the value of the U.S. dollar and addicted to U.S. consumer demand.

Even now, after the U.S. government's credit rating has been downgraded, investors are still flocking to the security of U.S. Treasury bonds. Why? Because the market for U.S. dollars remains the deepest and most liquid foreign exchange (forex) market in the world. The dollar is the currency of denomination for more than 60 percent of central banks' foreign reserves and 85 percent of all forex transactions worldwide.[10] The dollar's status as the world reserve currency thus allows the U.S. Treasury to pay much lower interest rates on the debt it issues because U.S. Treasury bonds are seen as very safe investments—the risk involved in buying U.S. debt (basically the risk that the United States will default on its debt) historically has been very low. However, perpetually low interest rates also mean that America's reserve currency status allows it to finance a ballooning national debt, even while showing few signs of emerging from its economic crisis.

Nonetheless, with the 2008 financial crisis and the unraveling of trillions of dollars in consumer debt in the years that followed, this time may have come to an end, just as the period of British economic dominance faded in the early twentieth century. Simply put, the buyer of last resort is exhausted. At present, the U.S. economy is overburdened with debt: corporate debt, household debt, and, to a lesser extent, government debt. The problems with debt management became overwhelming after the housing bubble burst in 2008 and sent America into a balance sheet recession. The nation's balance sheet had expanded over many years, in no small part because the United States used its "exorbitant privilege" of reserve currency status to finance its growing current account deficit in the period leading up to the financial crisis.

As a result, the United States is now looking at the end of its economic hegemony. And the world is facing another period of transition, in which the old dominant economic power cedes sole control to the new or, at the very least, shares control with the new in ways that it never has before. The trouble is that this next transformational phase will be much more challenging than the transition of power between the United Kingdom and the United States, two countries whose financial markets were at similar levels of development and structure and that shared cultural, legal, historical, and religious traditions. The gap between the United States and China today is much wider than the earlier gap between the United States and the United Kingdom, with the United States being at a far higher level of GDP per capita than China and with both countries evolving out of very different cultural traditions. These differences will make Sino-American economic and political interactions more fraught with tension than those between the United States and the United Kingdom. As a result, the relative decline of U.S. global leadership and the emergence of Chinese authority are likely to be much more difficult to evolve on a cooperative trajectory.

This is why China's currency policy is such a crucial diplomatic issue for the United States. While the dollar's status as a global reserve currency has kept the overall balance of payments stable, China's currency peg has had the effect of weakening the U.S. economy and imposing adjustment in the United States, where the exchange rate is too high and interest rates are too low. These currency imbalances are the lynchpin on which China's own economic success has been dependent. This weakening effect is most apparent during periods of significant underemployment, so a pegged RMB is especially detrimental as the United States faces a demand shortfall following the 2008 crisis.

In response, pressure has grown for U.S. policy makers to challenge China on its currency peg. China's economy serves to set the global price of labor, and many people in the developed world may come to share this antipathy toward China's heavily managed currency as it continues to pressure the manufacturing sectors of the West. This trend was evident at the 2011 G-20 conference, where the G-20 leaders issued a statement asking China to reconsider its currency peg.[11]

As the developed world faces domestic pressure amid national economic crises, it is not likely to allow China to continue funding its growth at the expense of the developed countries' welfare. And while China will probably become the world's largest economy and remain so for the foreseeable future, it is still dependent on access to export markets and on inflows of foreign direct investment and natural resources to fuel its growth. It must take international political developments into account when plotting its way forward. In today's fraught economic environment, China's current economic policy could create a situation in which other countries are forced to look after their own national interests more than global growth. The threat of a potential trade war still looms if China proves unwilling to begin allowing the RMB to appreciate. As South Korean President Lee Myung-bak said, "If the countries fail to reach an agreement and continue to seek their own interests, they will eventually see protectionism prevail across the world."[12] This "beggar thy neighbor" approach would be disastrous for the world economy, and its long-term effect would be to dampen growth—even in China.

After the Asian crisis in the late 1990s, other emerging nations followed China's lead and started accumulating large currency reserves in an attempt to insulate themselves from risk in the world economy. This was done with an eye toward preventing a repeat of the devastation caused by the shifts in foreign financial capital that occurred in 1997. For example, China's massive foreign reserves enabled the country to introduce an almost $600 billion stimulus package, which helped it mitigate the impact of the global economic slowdown.

But while large foreign currency reserves may be beneficial for one nation, this approach could be disastrous if many emerging nations continue attempting to do the same—and the size of the currency reserves in many of these countries, as well as the conservative nature of where those reserves are invested, suggest that they are. This could create a "paradox of risk aversion" similar to Keynes's paradox of thrift, whereby each country's attempts to insulate itself from risk serves, when taken collectively, to increase risk in the world economy, and in the end to actually increase that country's risk exposure.[13] By definition, not all countries can avoid risk in the current world economy, and a noncooperative approach is liable to make the present situation much worse. An inward-focused, mercantilist economy the size of China's will lead to lower growth for both China and the rest of the world. No one can afford a trade war, and a paradox of risk aversion could lead to an unnecessarily long and deep worldwide slump. It is in everyone's interest to find a new way forward.

Even without international pressure, China will eventually have to allow its currency to appreciate for domestic reasons. While China has managed its nominal exchange rate (the rate of exchange between the RMB and the U.S. dollar in the open market), its real exchange rate (how each currency is valued against the other after changes in prices in China and the United States are taken into account) is still appreciating. One way or another, either through nominal exchange-rate appreciation or through inflation-rate differentials caused by China's rapid growth and export-fueled economy, the Chinese real exchange rate will rise. Further, while China's foreign currency reserves helped it to weather the storm of the current crisis, maintaining more than $2.5 trillion in reserves represents an enormous misallocation of resources for a country in which most of the population remains very poor, living at just above subsistence levels.[14] China cannot invest all of its reserves at home, as this would lead to rapid increases in domestic inflation. And China does not have the capabilities to invest large sums of money overseas in anything but government securities, such as low-yield U.S. Treasury bonds. Even if China could do so, it's not clear that many countries would allow heavy Chinese investment, as China is still not considered a "friendly" country in much of the world because of suspicions regarding the different nature of its government.[15] In particular, developed countries and other developing nations that could support China's large-scale investments are wary of allowing a nondemocratically controlled China to gain significant influence in their domestic affairs. China's political history is still an impediment to its economic future.

Allowing the RMB to appreciate is also necessary if China is to make the transition from a manufacturing- and investment-dominated economy to a service- and consumer-driven economy. While China's undervalued exchange rate has helped its growth so far, this same policy may become a hindrance as China's economy evolves. From 2000 to 2010, investment has been growing at a far greater rate than consumption. The growth of fixed investment averaged 13.3 percent, while the growth of private consumption averaged only 7.8 percent. Over that same period, fixed investment increased from 34 percent to 46 percent of China's yearly GDP, while private consumption shrank from 46 percent of GDP to 34 percent.[16] If China is to transform its economy to a consumption-based model, this trend needs to be reversed. China's currency peg was a large part of what brought about this investment-led growth trend, since an artificially depreciated RMB suppressed wages, allowed for expansion of cheap credit, and repressed the exchange rate, all of which effectively transferred incomes from households to businesses, and thus from consumption to investment.[17]

However, this type of economic reorientation almost always leads to a significant, economy-wide deceleration in productivity growth, as nascent service industries exhibit much lower efficiency gains than China's manufacturing sector created during the major transition from agricultural to manufacturing production. To some degree, this kind of growth slowdown is unavoidable as China's economy matures. But recognizing this issue now could make the transition much smoother. A wise approach for China would be to begin making this change slowly and in a controlled manner, rather than allowing its currency to appreciate rapidly, as Japan did in the late 1980s, leading to economic stagnation.

The reality is that if China wants its economy to continue growing, one way or another it must begin facing the issues that its underappreciated currency has created. Real exchange-rate appreciation can be achieved through nominal exchange-rate appreciation, domestic inflation, or deflation in the rest of the world. The question is whether the pace of RMB appreciation will be fast enough for the rest of the world to be rescued from pressing deflation. And here the evidence is not encouraging.

Potential domestic resistance to RMB appreciation in China is ample. As George Soros has noted in the *Financial Times*, the government's discretion over the use of this surplus gives it a significant political edge in domestic and foreign policy issues. Given that most of the investment of surplus foreign reserves is handled directly or indirectly by the Chinese government, the domestic effect of a pegged RMB is essentially a tax on Chinese consumers that accrues to the government in the form of large currency reserves.[18] This strategy has had the effect of concentrating power in the hands of the Chinese leadership, both at home and abroad. Though the magnitude of China's current reserves glut means that additional inflows of surplus foreign reserves may not be necessary for the Chinese government to retain this influence, any shift away from China's currency peg may meet with significant resistance from China's entrenched bureaucratic elite. China's exporters, who gain a significant competitive advantage from an artificially deflated RMB, also are likely to resist RMB appreciation, and heavily leveraged state-owned enterprises (SOEs) and local governments are also likely to resist any attempt to allow the necessary rise in China's interest rates that would accompany a shift toward consumer-led growth.

The real challenge for China's leaders is that continuing the nation's currency peg is not necessarily in the long-term interests of the Chinese people. As noted earlier, this strategy has worked while China has been shifting its labor force from agriculture to manufacturing. But it is likely to be less effective later, when growth becomes more innovation-intensive and China's economy becomes more service-based.[19] Furthermore, if the world economy is to avoid the deflationary impact of Chinese mercantilist strategy and the possibility of a continuing crisis or collapse, then the Chinese government will be called upon to rebalance and give away some of the advantage that its currency peg provides. The Chinese government could, for example, aid the transition to a consumer-based economy by increasing government expenditures on healthcare, pensions, and education, which would boost private- and public-sector demand and indirectly support consumption by reducing the precautionary motive for household saving in China.[20]

China also could move its currency peg higher to allow the RMB to appreciate, lowering the effective "tax" on consumers of the current peg while also easing deflationary pressures in developed countries. This approach would help solve both domestic problems and international imbalances. However, it also would require the Chinese government to be willing to undertake a deliberate, long-term plan of action that would directly reduce its own bureaucratic control domestically and internationally and would challenge the profit margins of powerful coastal interests.

If China wishes to develop the deep and liquid capital markets necessary for its currency to serve as a store of value that is widely used abroad, it will first have to develop a strict rule of law with transparent court systems, which is currently nonexistent. Well-developed property rights would also be a necessity, as would robust financial regulatory authorities. But as one professor of economics at China's Beijing University has noted, "Almost everything [the Chinese government] has done, has been illegal" if it had strictly followed its own constitution. China's government has often forged ahead without regard to technical legality and revised the laws after the fact.[21] Foreign investors will be anxious about participating en masse in domestic Chinese currency markets if they lack confidence in the Chinese legal system. Yet, again, transforming the system to one of legal rules rather than bureaucratic discretion would mean a significant loss in political power for the Chinese government, and it is unclear whether the Chinese elites are willing or able to support that transformation.

To make matters even more complicated, there also are vested interests within the United States that resist RMB appreciation. The most notable advocates against Chinese currency reform are large U.S. corporations with direct investments in China that export their products back to the United States and low-cost American retailers like Walmart that benefit from the cheap labor that exists because of the pegged RMB. These companies are likely to oppose any attempt to get China's currency to appreciate, since it would directly harm their quarterly profits if Chinese wages were to rise in dollar terms.

But the U.S. business community is hardly monolithic on this issue. Indeed, there also is considerable pressure building on China to liberalize its currency from Western financial institutions, which want this change for their own pecuniary benefit. Wall Street financiers see the opening of the Chinese currency market as a potential windfall, since it would open an enormous new market for currency trading and the provision of a whole array of financial services that are well developed in the United States, so they are likely to continue to push China to open and deepen its financial markets for the foreseeable future. One need only look to the leading Chinese universities in economics and business education, where the boards are replete with Western financiers who are hoping to entice the children of the Chinese elite into finance, to understand that Wall Street and big finance have serious interests in China's financial deepening, which would be a precursor for currency convertibility. The result of this tug-of-war between Wall Street and multinational manufacturers and major retailers is likely to have a significant effect on U.S. policy regarding China in the future.

Despite Wall Street pressure, China is likely to avoid imitating the Western path of unbridled financialization and choose another road toward development. China is a country whose population is still about two-thirds rural—and in which 40 percent of the rural household budget is spent just on food.[22] This makes China very vulnerable to fluctuations in the RMB emanating from global currency markets. With such a large percentage of its population still living at near-subsistence levels, China can't afford to expose its population to the whims of volatile finance, especially given that the Communist Party's legitimacy seems to be dependent on the country's continued economic growth. China also is eminently aware of the lessons of the Japanese crash in the late 1980s and the ensuing lost decade that followed Japan's acquiescence to the exchange-rate appreciation demanded by the Western economic orthodoxy. The recent experience of the 1997 Asian crisis only served to reinforce distrust of Western financialization. Therefore, for reasons of both general interest and elite self-interest, China is likely to resist full capital account liberalization.

China is walking on a knife's edge between domestic imperatives and the impact that its size and policies have on the rest of the world. If China proves to be unwilling to change its current currency policy, its intransigence could well drive the world economy into a prolonged slump that worsens the credit crises in the United States and Europe. This could lead to financial and banking failures that could then spread the recession to the developing world—China included. European banks alone have extended credit of more than US$3 trillion to the emerging world. A drying up of that credit in debt deflation would weaken Eastern Europe, Latin America, the Middle East, and Asia. As the logic of the paradox of risk aversion suggests, by trying to insulate itself from risk, the Chinese government could well increase both its country's and the world's exposure to the risk of political and economic dysfunction.

This may explain why, despite China's resistance to exchange-rate adjustments, there are some recent signs pointing to an awareness of the dangers posed by its currency policy. In a strategy very similar to the one employed by the United States in the early twentieth century, China appears to be running experiments and exploring the benefits of the eventual use of its currency as an international reserve currency. The emergence of the RMB as an international reserve currency would enable Chinese firms and investors to limit their foreign exchange exposures as a result of being able to carry out international transactions in their own currency. Chinese banks would be better able to compete for international business, helping to develop Shanghai as an international financial center by bringing its banks a substantial share of the global foreign exchange market.[23] And China's central bank would be able to follow a nonpegged monetary policy that could help foster further domestic growth.[24] These benefits are ample, and it appears that China may be starting to become interested in pursuing them.

Since 2009, China has suggested that it will slowly begin to move in a new direction, demonstrating its intention to internationalize the RMB, supposedly within a decade. While this may seem unlikely today, it is worth remembering that in the early twentieth century, the U.S. dollar went from a complete nonfactor to dominance in global currency markets in only 10 years.[25] China has begun allowing the RMB to be used in trade-related transactions and has entered into bilateral agreements with other countries, the largest being Brazil, to allow the RMB to be used in trade there. More than 70,000 companies are now doing cross-border settlements in RMB.[26] In 2004, banks in Hong Kong were allowed to accept RMB deposits. In January 2011, the Bank of China was allowed to provide RMB deposit accounts in New York and to use the RMB in bilateral U.S.-China trade.

But despite these modest efforts, China is still a long way from having full currency convertibility and deep and liquid RMB markets. While China has played with allowing the RMB to serve as a medium of exchange, as well as its existing role as a unit of account, in the short term, China seems to be unwilling to allow its currency to become a store of value similar to the dollar. And, as noted earlier, the country does not yet have the deep and liquid financial markets or the robust courts and financial regulation that are prerequisites for full currency convertibility. Change on either of these fronts will require the Chinese government to give up considerable control. So progress will probably be very slow.

The reality facing the West is that China is already one of the major powers in the global economy. In the near future, it is certain to share the world stage with the United States. It is possible that within a few decades, China's RMB will emerge as an international currency. This could happen even sooner if the Chinese government truly commits itself to the project of currency liberalization. In the 1920s, the United States was able to achieve the transformation in just a decade largely because the recently created Federal Reserve Bank backed the market in bank acceptances, providing liquidity for the market even though the Fed often lost money on the transactions.[27] So now it's China's turn to put its foot forward.

Perhaps the most important question facing society today is: What will this new world look like as China's presence on the global stage grows? It is theoretically possible that China's RMB could take over as the leading global reserve currency, replacing the U.S. dollar altogether, if the United States proves to be unable to address its growing domestic tensions and problems. But this is unlikely to happen, and it isn't a particularly desirable outcome for the global economy. The benefits to the network from having a single global reserve currency are probably not sufficient to keep one currency dominant. This logic suggests that there is room for more than one global currency. Indeed, historically there has typically been more than one reserve currency. For example, the U.S. dollar and the U.K.

pound sterling shared this precise role for several decades until the mid-twentieth century.[28]

Replacing the dollar with the RMB would not solve the problems that the current system faces. It would do little to correct the global imbalances that such single-reserve systems cause. Further, it is not clear that central banks would want one dominant reserve currency because diversification to a multi-polar approach could lead to enhanced stability in global foreign exchange markets compared to the current structure, which features substantial dollar-denominated overhangs. This approach would not have the control of a centralized world currency the way a retooled Special Drawing Right (SDR) created by the International Monetary Fund (IMF) would. But it would have the advantage of being politically feasible. SDRs or some other global unit of account would be unlikely to gain international approval. Historically, international institutions like the IMF have been deliberately restricted from carrying out precisely the functions that would be required of them if they were to maintain an international currency, and currently there are no other institutions available to fill this role.[29]

Of course, this points to the fundamental problem in the global economy: the world's major powers are unlikely to grant to any truly international institution the kind of control necessary for maintaining a global currency. This reticence is visible in the struggles of the European Union, where many member nations—particularly the surplus nations like Germany—were hesitant to give the European Community and the European Central Bank full control over fiscal and monetary policy. (And lest we forget, China, the world's biggest surplus nation, would probably act no differently in similar circumstances.) Therefore, it is unlikely that an even more creative understanding could be reached by an even larger collection of countries with fewer cultural, historical, or political ties.

The most likely outcome, then, is a world in which several global currencies exist at once, probably the RMB, the dollar, and the euro, if Europe can save itself from itself. Under this scenario, the main challenge for the United States would be whether it can fix its domestic problems. Can America rebuild its crumbling domestic infrastructure and education system and correct the extreme imbalances in income and wealth distribution? If it can't, it is unlikely that the United States will be able to continue its dominant role on the global stage. The United States still enjoys large advantages in key areas, such as high-tech development and global cultural influence. But suddenly they are America's to lose.

For China, the main challenge is to get the world to accommodate its success. If China is not economically dominant in 30 years, it will probably be because it could not achieve a cooperative understanding for a system that works with both the developed and the emerging worlds. This outcome is not desirable to anyone involved because it would cause the global economy to operate at a much lower level of per capita income, employment, and wealth than would otherwise be possible.[30] In the near future, the growth of the world economy is likely to be driven by China. Therefore, limiting China's growth will have substantial adverse feedback effects on everyone else. It is in the entire world's long-term best interest that China's economy continues to grow and develop at a healthy rate. But China also must be sensitive to the exigencies of international politics because potential trade and currency wars are likely to lead down this road as well.

In the short term, China is not likely to make its currency fully convertible (freely exchangeable without government restriction). The Japanese collapse, the 1997 Asian crisis, and the 2008 financial crisis have demonstrated the potential calamities that await a system based on unfettered short-term capital mobility. But China is likely to begin to change its currency peg, slowly moving it up to allow the RMB to appreciate against the dollar. The hope is that China will do this at a rate that will produce positive effects for struggling developed nations and keep China's economy growing and stable. In the long term, this move in China's currency regime also is necessary if China is to make the transition to a more service- and high-tech-oriented economy.

What the world is facing, ultimately, is what Mohamad El-Erian, the head of the asset management firm PIMCO, has called a "non-cooperative cooperative game." It is unlikely that implementing any sweeping global financial architecture like a true world currency will be politically feasible in the near future. Therefore, countries must continue to try to generate better cooperative outcomes in an ad hoc manner, often without working together directly. The potential pitfalls of this situation are demonstrated in the paradox of risk aversion, where a country that pursues only its own short-term interest in an attempt to insulate itself from risk can actually hurt its own economy after the repercussions that its actions impose on other economies affect the home country. The world's leading countries, China in particular, must heighten the weight they give to how their domestic interests affect other nations. They must begin to realize that their own long-term economic health is contingent upon the success of the worldwide economy.

The vast web of global trade and commerce that exists today and that benefits people the world over evolved through just such an uncooperative game. But it also is instructive to remember the catastrophes that the current system has produced.

China is, perhaps rightly, leery of Western economic and political policies that historically have been used to promote the short-term interests of Western financial elites at the expense of the well-being of those in developing (and, often enough, also developed) countries In many ways, the current Chinese currency peg and buildup of substantial foreign currency reserves can be seen as a direct reaction to the disasters that those Western policies brought upon the East. Going forward, it will be important to keep in mind who benefits from these policies. One must ask not only, "What does it do?" but also, "Who is it for?"

It also will be important to keep an eye on the competing forces of national governments, local populations, domestic manufacturing interests, and global financial elites. To some degree, the debate must shift from economics to politics. As the economist Michael Pettis does well to note, "The process of adjustment is a political one."[31] The changes that are taking place both in the world economy and in China's domestic economy are happening and will happen. The real question is, who will bear the burdens of these changes —and who will benefit from them? This, first and foremost, is a political question and a question of political power.

In practice, the route forward will not be decided simply by technocratic questions about the best possible results. Any look at future outcomes in the global economic system must keep in mind the realities of political economy. This is as true in Europe and the United States as it is in China. Whose interests win out will ultimately determine the path that we take. In this light, the challenges ahead for China and the rest of the world are considerable. Whether or not we succeed will depend on how the constellation of interests that is at play in the global economic system forges ahead. For things to work out well, the microinterests that have led to the current colossal imbalances will need to move in a constructive direction. It is possible that we will find success. But it is also possible that the entire system will deteriorate under the weight of its own contradictions. There is a way. We will find out if there is the will.

REFERENCES

Chapter 3

Baldwin, R. "In or Out: Does It Matter? An Evidence-Based Analysis of the Euro's Trade Effects." Centre for Economic Policy Research, London, 2006.

Bénassy-Quéré, A., and J. Pisani-Ferry. "What International Monetary System for a Fast-Changing World Economy?" Working Paper 2011–04b, CEPII Research Center, Paris, 2011.

Bundesbank. "European Economic and Monetary Union." Frankfurt am Main, 2008.

De Grauwe, P. "The Euro at Ten—Achievements and Challenges." Paper presented at the annual meeting of the Austrian Economic Association, Vienna, 2008.

Duisenberg, W. F. "The Past and the Future of European Integration: A Central Banker's Perspective." 1999 Per Jacobsson Lecture, Washington, DC, 2008.

ECB. "European Integration." 2011, http://www.ecb.int/ecb/educational/facts/euint/html/ei_007.en.html, accessed October 7, 2011.

Eichengreen, B. "The Bear of Bretton Woods." Project Syndicate, Berkeley, CA, 2011.

Eichengreen, B., "The Dollar Dilemma—The World's Top Currency Faces Competition", *Foreign Affairs*, Vol. 88, No. 5 (September/October 2009).

Eichengreen, B. "Sterling's Past, Dollar's Future: Historical Perspectives on Reserve Currency Competition." NBER Working Paper No. 11336, National Bureau of Economic Research, Cambridge, MA, 2005.

Eichengreen, B., and M. Flandreau. "The Rise and Fall of the Dollar, or When Did the Dollar Replace Sterling as the Leading Reserve Currency?" *European Review of Economic History* 13 (2009).

European Commission. "European Economic Forecast." Brussels, Spring 2011.

European Commission. "Standard Eurobarometer 73." Brussels, 2010.

Ghosh, A. R., J. D. Ostry, and C. Tsangarides. "Exchange-Rate Regimes and the Stability of the International Monetary System," International Monetary Fund, Washington, DC, 2010.

Heipertz, M., and A. Verdun. *Ruling Europe: The Politics of the Stability and Growth Pact.* Cambridge, U.K.: Cambridge University Press, 2010.

IMF "Factsheet 'Special Drawing Rights' (SDR)." International Monetary Fund, Washington, DC, 2012.

IMF. "Spillover Report on the Euro Area." International Monetary Fund, Washington, DC, 2011a.

IMF. "Spillover Report on the USA." International Monetary Fund, Washington, DC, 2011b.

IMF. "Article IV Report on the Euro Area." International Monetary Fund, Washington, DC, 2011c.

IMF. "Reserve Accumulation and International Monetary Stability." International Monetary Fund, Washington, DC, 2010.

Kern, A. "Sovereign Debt Restructuring in the EU: Lessons from the Recent Crisis." In P. Delimatsis and N. Herger (eds.), *Financial Regulation at the Crossroads*. Leiden: Kluwer Law International, 2011.

Le Cacheux, J., and F. Touya. "The Dismal Record of the Stability and Growth Pact." In I. Linsenmann, et al. (eds.), *Economic Government of the EU—A Balance Sheet of New Modes of Policy Coordination*. Houndmills, U.K.: Palgrave Macmillan, 2007.

Lim. 2010.

Lim, E-G. "The Euro's Challenge to the Dollar: Different Views from Economists and Evidence from COFER and Other Data." IMF Working Paper 06/153, International Monetary Fund, Washington, DC, 2006.

Mateos y Lago et al. 2010.

Mateos y Lago, I., et al. "The Debate on the International Monetary System." IMF Staff Position Note, International Monetary Fund, Washington, DC, 2009.

McKinnon, R. I. *The World Dollar Standard and Globalization, New Rules for the Game?* Stanford, CA: Stanford University Press, 2005.

Meissner, C., and N. Oomes. (2008). "Why Do Countries Peg the Way They Peg? The Determinants of Anchor Currency Choice," IMF Working Paper 08/132,IMF, Washington, DC.

Micco, A., E. Stein, and G. Ordoñez. "The Currency Union Effect on Trade: Early Evidence from EMU." Inter-American Development Bank, Washington, DC, 2003.

Mongelli, F. P., and C. Wyplosz. "The Euro at Ten: Unfulfilled Threats and Unexpected Challenges." In B. Maćkowiak et al. (eds.), *The Euro at Ten—Lessons and Challenges*, Frankfurt am Main, Germany: ECB, 2009.

Ortiz Martínez, G. "Panel Statement." In B. Maćkowiak et al. (eds.), *The Euro at Ten—Lessons and Challenges.* Frankfurt am Main, Germany: ECB, 2009.

Papademos, L. "Opening Address." In B. Maćkowiak et al. (eds.), *The Euro at Ten—Lessons and Challenges.* Frankfurt am Main, Germany: ECB, 2009.

Pisani-Ferry, J., and A. Sapir. "Euro Area: Ready for the Storm?" In J. Pisani-Ferry and A. S. Posen (eds.), *The Euro at Ten: The Next Global Currency?* Brussels: Peterson Institute for International Economics, 2009.

Prasad, E. *Role Reversal in Global Finance.* Washington, DC: Brookings Institution, 2011.

Prati, A., and G. J. Schinasi. "European Monetary Union and International Capital Markets: Structural Implications and Risks." IMF Working Paper No. 97/62, International Monetary Fund, Washington, DC, 1997.

Rodrik, Dani. *The Globalisation Paradox.* W.W. Norton & Company, New York, 2011.

Wall, S. "Joining the Euro: Not Just Britain's Place in Europe, but Europe's in the World." In J. Stevens, *10 Years of the Euro: Perspectives for Britain.* London: Sarum Colorview, 2008.

Chapter 6

Aziz, J., and L. Cui. "Explaining China's Low Consumption: The Neglected Role of Household Income." IMF Working Paper No. 07/181 (Washington, DC: International Monetary Fund, 2007).

Bai, C., and Z. Qian. "Factor Income Share in China: The Story Behind the Statistics." *China Economic Journal* 2 (2009).

Barnett, S., and R. Brooks. "Does Government Spending on Health and Education Raise Consumption?" Chapter 7 in *Rebalancing Growth in Asia*, edited by V. Arora and R. Cardarelli (Washington, DC: International Monetary Fund, 2010).

Blanchard, O., and F. Giavazzi. "Rebalancing Growth in China: A Three Handed Approach." CEPR Discussion No. 5403 (London: Center for Economic Policy Research, 2005).

Geng, N., and P. N'Diaye. "Determinants of Corporate Investment in China: Evidence from Cross Country Firm-Level Data." IMF Working Paper (forthcoming), 2011.

Guo, K., and P. N'Diaye. "Is China's Export-Oriented Growth Sustainable?" IMF Working Paper No. 09/172 (Washington, DC: International Monetary Fund, 2009).

Huang, Y. "China's Great Ascendancy and Structural Risks: Consequences of Asymmetric Market Liberalization." *Asian-Pacific Economic Literature* 24 (2010), pp. 65–85.

Huang, Y., and K. Y. Tao, "Causes and Remedies of China's External Imbalances." China Center for Economic Research Working Paper 2010–02, 2010.

Kujis, L. "Investment and Saving in China," Policy Research Working Paper No. 3633 (Washington, DC: World Bank, 2005).

Modigliani, F., and S. L. Cao. "The Chinese Saving Puzzle and the Life Cycle Hypothesis," *Journal of Economic Literature* 42, No 1 (2004), pp. 145–170.

Mohammad, A., P. N'Diaye, and O. Unteroberdoerster. "Rebalancing Growth in Asia." Chapter 1 in *Rebalancing Growth in Asia*, edited by V. Arora and R. Cardarelli (Washington, DC: International Monetary Fund, 2010).

Wei, S., and X. Zhang. "The Competitive Saving Motive: Evidence from Rising Sex Ratios and Savings Rates in China." NBER Working Paper No. 15093 (Cambridge, MA: National Bureau of Economic Research, 2009).

NOTES

Preface

1. http://www.ft.com/intl/cms/s/0/eda8f512-eaae-11df-b28d-00144feab49a.html#axzz1yvtyoj3P

Chapter 3

1. This contribution was written in my capacity as State Secretary at the German Federal Ministry of Finance (2008–2011), i.e., before I became a Member of the Executive Board of the European Central Bank (January 2012). I would like to thank Johannes Wolff, Christian Dalhaus, and Dr. Rouven Klein from the staff of the Federal Ministry of Finance for assisting me in the research for this article and their valuable contributions in discussing the subject matter.
2. This section is an edited and abbreviated version of information provided by the Bundesbank (Bundesbank, 2008).
3. For a more detailed assessment of the euro's role as a reserve currency in a multipolar currency system, see also "The Future" section of this chapter.

Chapter 6

1. The views expressed herein are those of the authors and should not be attributed to the International Monetary Fund, its executive board, or its management.
2. See Mohammad, N'Diaye, and Unteroberdoerster (2010).
3. See Geng and N'Diaye (forthcoming).
4. See Huang (2010) and Huang and Tao (2010).
5. Typically found in markets with very few sellers.
6. See Blanchard and Giavazzi (2005), Kujis (2005), Modigliani and Cao (2004), Aziz and Cui (2007), Wei and Zhang (2009), and Bai and Qian (2009).
7. Lending rates are subject to a floor, and deposit rates are subject to a ceiling.

Chapter 7

1. See James Rickards, *Currency Wars: The Making of the Next Global Crisis* (New York: Portfolio/Penguin, 2011).
2. Ibid.
3. Guido Mantega as quoted in Jonathan Wheatley, "Brazil in 'Currency War' Alert," *Financial Times*, September 27, 2010.
4. "Currency Composition of Official Foreign Exchange Reserves," International Monetary Fund, Washington, DC, http://www.imf.org/external/np/sta/cofer/eng/cofer.pdf. March, 2012.
5. Ibid.
6. Barry Eichengreen, *Exorbitant Privilege: The Rise and Fall of the Dollar and the Future of the International Monetary System* (New York, Oxford University Press, 2011).

7. "Enhancing International Monetary Stability—A Role for the SDR?," International Monetary Fund, Washington, DC, January 2011, http://www.imf.org/external/np/pp/eng/2011/010711.pdf.

8. "Factsheet, Special Drawing Rights (SDRs)," International Monetary Fund, Washington, DC, September 13, 2011, http://www.imf.org/external/ np/exr/facts/sdr.ht.

Chapter 8

1. Timothy Green, *The Ages of Gold* (London: Thomson Reuters GFMS, 2007), p. 29.

2. Ibid., p. 187.

3. Christopher Howgego, "The Supply and Use of Money in the Roman World, 200 BC–AD 300," *Journal of Roman Studies* 82 (1992), pp. 1–31.

4. Green, *The Ages of Gold*, p. 187.

5. Ibid., p. 241.

6. John Maynard Keynes, *The Economic Consequences of the Peace* (1919) http://www.econlib.org/library/YPDBooks/Keynes/kynsCP.html page VI.14.

Chapter 9

1. Brett Arends, "IMF Bombshell: Age of America Nears End," *MarketWatch*, April 25, 2011, http://www.marketwatch.com/story/imf-bombshell-age-of-america-about-to-end-2011-04-25.

2. *World Economic Outlook, April 2011*, International Monetary Fund, Washington, DC, http://www.imf.org/external/pubs/ft/weo/2011/01/.

3. Ibid.; calculated in purchasing power parity (PPP) terms.
4. Giles Chance, *China and the Credit Crisis: The Emergence of a New World Order* (Hoboken, NJ: John Wiley & Sons, 2010), p. 182.
5. C. Fred Bergsten, "The Dollar and the Renminbi," May 23, 2007, http://www.iie.com/publications/testimony/testimony.cfm?ResearchID=747.
6. Bureau of Economic Analysis, U.S. International Transactions.
7. Paul Krugman, "Trade and Wages, Reconsidered," February 2008, http://www.princeton.edu/~pkrugman/pk-bpea-draft.pdf.
8. David H. Autor, David Dorn, and Gordon H. Hanson, "The China Syndrome: Local Labor Market Effects of Import Competition in the United States," May 2012, http://economics.mit.edu/files/6613.
9. Ibid.
10. Barry Eichengreen, "Why the Dollar's Reign Is Near an End," *Wall Street Journal*, March 1, 2011.
11. Daniel Flynn and Noah Barkin, "G20 Names China in Call for Greater FX Flexibility," Reuters, November 4, 2011, http://www.reuters.com/article/2011/11/04/us-g20-plan-idUSTRE7A31KQ20111104.
12. Na Jeong-ju, "China Should Let Yuan Appreciate for World," *Korea Times*, October 21, 2010, http://www.koreatimes.co.kr/www/news/biz/2010/10/127_74947.html.
13. Robert Johnson, "A Paradox of Risk Aversion: Structural Uncertainty and a Dysfunctional International Monetary System," *Challenge* 54, No. 3 (May/June 2011), pp. 38–55.
14. Bergsten, "The Dollar and the Renminbi."

15. Carl E. Walter, "China's Reserves Are Worthless Because They Can't Use Them," China Boom, http://chinaboom. asiasociety.org/period/overdrive/0/233.
16. Martin Wolf, "How China Could Yet Fail Like Japan," *Financial Times*, June 14, 2011, http://www.ft.com/intl/cms/s/0/6247d8e2-96b8-11e0-baca-00144feab49a.html.
17. Ibid.
18. George Soros, "China Must Fix the Global Currency Crisis," *Financial Times*, October 7, 2010, http://www.ft.com/intl/cms/s/0/f4dd9122-d22a-11df-8fbe-00144feabdc0.html#axzz1x23A4W14.
19. Wolf, "How China Could Yet Fail Like Japan."
20. Bergsten, "The Dollar and the Renminbi."
21. Yao Yang, "Almost Everything We've Done Is Illegal," China Boom, http://chinaboom.asiasociety.org/period/prospects/0/176.
22. Chance, *China and the Credit Crisis*, p. 181.
23. Barry Eichengreen, "What China Is After Financially," East Asia Forum, January 30, 2011, http://www.eastasiaforum.org/2011/01/30/what-china-is-after-financially/.
24. Barry Eichengreen, "The Renminbi as an International Currency," January 2010, http://cmlab.berkeley.edu/~eichengr/renminbi_international_1–2011.pdf.
25. Barry Eichengreen and Marc Flandreau, "The Federal Reserve, the Bank of England, and the Rise of the Dollar as an International Currency, 1914–39," BIS Working Paper no. 329, November 2010.
26. Eichengreen, "What China Is After Financially."
27. Eichengreen and Flandreau, "The Federal Reserve."
28. Ibid.

29. Martin Wolf, video discussion at Peterson Institute of *Eclipse: Living in the Shadow of China's Economic Dominance*, by Arvind Subramanian, http://www.piie.com/events/event_detail.cfm?EventID=198&Media.

30. Mohamed A. El-Erian, video discussion at Peterson Institute of *Eclipse*, http://www.piie.com/events/event_detail.cfm?EventID=198&Media.

31. Michael Pettis, "Some Predictions for the Rest of the Decade," China Financial Markets, http://mpettis.com/2011/08/some-predictions-for-the-rest-of-the-decade/.

INDEX

f indicates figure

Alexander the Great, 5, 10
American Business (C. Jackson Grayson, Jr., and Carla O'Dell), 10–11
Apple, 36
Arabian dinar, 4, 24, 29, 202–203
Arabs, ancient, 5
Asia:
    export value added in GDP, 166*f*
    factors in GDP growth, 164, 164*f*
    future preeminence of, 144
    potential reserve currency from country in, 88
    U.S. dollar status in, 80
Asian central banks, 85, 86
Asian crisis (1997-1998), 47, 84
    currency reserves accumulation after, 226–227
    and role of IMF, 193–194
Asmussen, Jörg, *v*
Athenian drachma, 5
Athens, ancient, 5
Australia:
    GDP per hour worked in, 33*f*
    productivity growth in, 31*f*
Austria, 9
    in EMU, 98
    GDP per hour worked in, 33*f*
    productivity growth in, 31*f*

Balance of payments crises, 110–111
Banfield, Edward, 132
Banfield, Laura, 132
Bank for International Settlements (BIS), 80
Bank loans, in China, 46–47
Bank of England, balance sheet of, 214*f*
Banks:
    eurozone country banks, 9, 28, 60, 136–137
    forex trades of, *xix–xx*
    (*See also* Central banks)
Barre Plan, 92

Basel Accord, 93
Belgium:
    in EMU, 98
    GDP per hour worked in, 33*f*
    government expenditures in, 140*f*
    productivity growth in, 31*f*
    productivity in, 19
Bernanke, Ben, 1, 126, 198, 211, 212, 217
BIS (Bank for International Settlements), 80
Bismarck, Otto von, 134
Bolivia, gold bought by, 214
Boockvar, Peter, *v*
Brazil:
    future role of, 120
    in G-20, 190
    GDP of, 120
    in global economic decisions, *xii*
    gold bought by, 214
    money pouring into, *xiii*
Brazilian real, *xxii*
Breadth of markets:
    and success as international currency, 22
    and the U.S. dollar, 44, 45*f*
Bretton Woods Agreement, *xiv, xvii–xix*, 208–209
    fixed-exchange-rate system of, 92, 192
    and gold standard, 208–209
    IMF created by, 192
    and modern currency issues, 127
BRIC nations:
    in global economic decisions, *xii*
    money pouring into, *xiii*
    (*See also individual nations*)
British pound sterling:
    as early trade and reserve currency, 6–7
    fall against the dollar, 20
    and gold standard, 24
    preeminent role in world order, *xviii*
    as reserve currency, 29, 114, 131*f*
    reserves held in, 82, 82*f*, 101*f*, 117*f*
    worldwide use of, 112

253

Dollar:
  Spanish, 6
  U.S. (*see* U.S. dollar)
Drachma, 5
Drachma, Athenian, 5
Draghi, Mario, 145, 152
Dual international currencies, 29–30
Ducat (ducato), Venetian, 6, 203
Dutch country banks, 9
Dutch guilder, 6, 13

ECB (*see* European Central Bank)
Ecofin Council (Council of Economic and
  Finance Ministers), 95–96, 98
The Economic Consequences of the Peace (John
  Maynard Keynes), 207–208
Economic growth:
  in China, 53, 74, 161–185, 174*f*, 220–221,
    229–233
    addressing present imbalances,
      175–184, 176*f*
    benefits of, 184–185
    and corporate savings, 171, 171*f*
    and current growth model, 161–163,
      183–184
    and dependence on external demand,
      164–166, 164*f*, 166*f*, 167*f*
    and employment growth, 173, 174*f*
    financial-sector reform, 177–180
    healthcare, pensions, and education
      reforms, 177
    and household consumption, 172–173,
      172*f*
    input costs and corporate reforms, 180
    and investment, 167–170, 168*f*–170*f*
    limits on, 37–39
    present economic imbalances,
      163–164
    and service sector, 173, 174*f*
    yuan appreciation, 180–184, 181*f*
  global, 189–190
  for success as international currency,
    21–22
  in the U.S., 35
Economic policies:
  of China, 50, 52–53, 222, 226
  of Europe
    and EMU first stage, 95–96
    and EMU reform, 106–107
    and EMU second stage, 96–98
  as tools, 133–134
Economic size:
  of China, 36
  and hegemonic reserve currency, 74–76
  and success as international currency, 22

and the U.S. dollar, 36–44, 37*f*, 38*f*, 40*f*,
  41*f*, 43*f*, 44*f*
Economies of scale, 77
Economy, world (*see* World economy)
ECU (European Currency Unit), 82, 82*f*
Education reforms, for China, 177
EEC (European Economic Community),
  10, 92
Egypt, ancient, 10, 202
Eichengreen, Barry, 196
El-Erian, Mohamad, 238
EMCF (European Monetary Cooperation
  Fund), 93
Emerging economies:
  and changing world power dynamic,
    xxiii
  effect of U.S. and European economies
    on, 68
Emerging nations:
  Asian, 144
  and competitive devaluation, *xiii*
Emerging-market economies:
  future role of, 120
  official reserves held by, 84
  self-insurance by central banks of, 75n.2
EMI (European Monetary institute), 96
Employment:
  in China, 46
  in the U.S., 35, 36
EMS (European Monetary System), 94
EMU (*see* European Economic and
  Monetary Union)
The End of History and the Last Man (Francis
  Fukuyama), 125–126
Energy, in China, 168–169, 169*f*
England:
  gold in, 206–207
  productivity in, 19
  recent inflation in, 212
EPU (European Payments Union), 92
ESFS (European Financial Stability Facility),
  107–108, 153–154
ESM (European Stability Mechanism),
  108–109, 153–154
ESRB (European Systemic Risk Board), 108
Estonia:
  GDP per hour worked in, 33*f*
  productivity growth in, 30, 31*f*
EU (European Union), 9, 142
EU Stability and Growth Pact, 60–62
Euro, 91–124
  benefits of, 102–103
  criteria for introducing, 98
  current trends in reserve status of,
    113–114, 113*f*

ABOUT THE EDITOR

Sara Eisen is a correspondent for Bloomberg Television and appears daily on *Bloomberg Surveillance*, Bloomberg's TV program that begins the day's conversation on business, economics, finance and investment. She also can be seen daily on Bloomberg TV's *Lunch Money* mid-day program. Based in New York City, Eisen specializes in covering global macroeconomics, with a focus on foreign exchange and fixed income markets. She has extensively covered the European debt crisis, interviewing top political leaders and finance ministers from Germany to Greece; she also frequently moderates panels on international economics.